THE ICONIC NORDIC HOUSE

THE ICONIC NORDIC HOUSE

MODERN MASTERWORKS SINCE 1900

Dominic Bradbury
Photography by Richard Powers

CONTENTS

Introduction

The revealing red thread that ties Nordic architecture together can be seen in the deep-rooted respect across the region for the beauty of the natural world. There are, of course, many ingredients that connect these northern countries, with their shared histories, yet it is the landscape above all that unites them. Across Scandinavia, the mountains, islands, forests and fjords can be extreme, as can the weather, but these elements are also rich in every regard, inspiring wonder and delight. Nordic architects have traditionally designed houses and buildings with such settings at the forefront of their imaginations, and this is still true of twentieth- and twenty-first-century practices for whom context is everything.

Norwegian master architect Sverre Fehn spoke of the importance of understanding the genius loci, or the spirit of a place. His work, along with that of many of his contemporaries, was grounded in an appreciation of nature. 'The physical ground means a lot to me,' he once said, and 'the building's relationship to the earth. In the Norwegian reality, you stand there upon the earth and you don't really have anything else, for realizing your conceptions in relation to, but nature. The intellectual world encounters the landscape and in this duel which arises, beauty is born.'[1]

Such encounters have given rise to the unique houses and homes of the Scandinavian countries, including the iconic exemplars explored within the pages of this book, which carry through from the early years of the twentieth century up until today. These are site-specific and original residences that touch the earth lightly, yet also offer a wealth of inspiration that spreads way beyond their original ambition and intent.

This story begins with Carl and Karin Larsson's extraordinary house in Sundborn, Sweden, known as Lilla Hyttnäs, or 'little cabin' (1890/1900/1912; see p. 16). At the turn of the century, the Larssons created a family home that fused past and present, art and design,

Carl & Karin Larsson's Lilla Hyttnäs, Sundborn, Sweden, 1890/1900/1912.

The circular living room on the upper level of Erik Gunnar Asplund's Villa Snellman, Djursholm, Sweden, 1918.

as well as house, garden and landscape. The couple used their rural retreat, which evolved gradually over time, as a canvas for their work and, more than this, translated their design philosophy into a beautifully illustrated lifestyle manual, *Ett Hem*, or *At Home*, first published in 1899 and reprinted many times over. The Larssons not only tied their home and their art to nature, but were also among the first to explicitly express a lifestyle philosophy that was truly Scandinavian and Nordic. It took account of the landscape, the changing seasons and the importance of family and friends, yet also placed the idea of 'home' at the centre of all these themes.

During the early decades of the twentieth century, architects and designers such as Eliel Saarinen, Erik Gunnar Asplund and Josef Frank also explored the fascinating hinterland between tradition and modernity. They drew on the vernacular, as well as romanticism and classicism, yet designed houses that were key staging posts on the journey towards modernism itself. In doing so, again landscape, context and the natural world were all important. Pioneering Finnish architect Eliel Saarinen, for example, settled not in Helsinki but on the shores of Lake Vitträsk to the west of the city, where he created both a family home and an architectural studio, known simply as Hvitträsk (1903; see p. 24). Here, again, the surroundings were key to the composition and conception of the house, which always managed to be cohesive and engaging while drawing on a wide range of references and points of inspiration.

> During the early decades of the twentieth century, architects such as Eliel Saarinen, Erick Gunnar Asplund and Josef Frank explored the fascinating hinterland between tradition and modernity.

The great figurehead of twentieth-century northern architecture, certainly in relation to the subject of contextual design created as a response to the landscape, was Alvar Aalto. Like Frank Lloyd Wright in the United States, Aalto developed a carefully considered version of modern organic architecture, which was highly responsive to site and setting. Yet Aalto's responses were also decidedly Scandinavian, as seen – above all – at Villa Mairea (1939; see p. 54), set among the pine forests of Noormarkku in Finland.

Here, Aalto brought nature into the house itself. He made the most of warm, characterful natural materials, while the wooden columns and supports around the entrance hall and staircase echoed the trunks of the trees outside. Picture windows framed the garden vista and Aalto added a winter garden and integrated planters, bringing flora and fauna into the home. At the same time, Villa Mairea was a truly innovative modernist accomplishment, rich in ideas, with its great, open-plan living room and fluid floor plan. The architect and

his clients sincerely believed that good, modern architecture could make the world a better place, with Villa Mairea designed not only as a family home but as an exemplar of what might be possible.

Importantly, Aalto was also one of the great Scandinavian polymaths. Like Arne Jacobsen and Finn Juhl, he was not only an architect but also an inventor of interiors and furniture, who saw architecture within the wider context of design more generally. Aalto, Jacobsen and Juhl were also the authors of some of the most famous and enduring furniture designs of the mid-century period, which brought their work to a much wider and more international audience.

During the post-war period, these Nordic modern masters and many others, such as Jørn Utzon and Viljo Revell, forged the ideal of 'warm modernism', or 'soft modernism', which offered an enticing and more expressive alternative to the limitations of the International Style. There was a clear willingness to experiment and

Above Mork-Ulnes's Skigard Hytte in Kvitfjell, Norway, 2019.

Opposite Views of the Lysefjord from a Star Lodge designed by Snøhetta at The Bolder, Forsand, Norway, 2023.

Following pages The sauna at Manshausen Sea Cabins, Manshausen Island, Norway, designed by Snorre Stinessen, 2015. PK Arkitektar's Árborg Villa, Árborg, Iceland, 2009.

innovate, as seen in the work of designers such as Yrjö Kukkapuro, Antti and Vuokko Nurmesniemi, as well as Matti Suuronen, inventor of the prefabricated Space Age dwelling known as Futuro House (1968; see p. 124) in Finland. The combination of ambition and experimentation can also be seen in many of the more contemporary houses featured in the book, such as Espen Surnevik's PAN Cabin Three (2018; see p. 246) and Snøhetta's clifftop escapes at The Bolder (2023; see p. 302), both in Norway, or the extraordinary Villa Gug (2022; see p. 294) in Denmark by Bjarke Ingels's practice, BIG.

As well as the ongoing relationship between architecture and landscape, the book explores a number of other key themes, which carry all the way through the northern nations. There are engaging cabins and rural escapes arranged over the following pages, and the continuing dialogue between art and architecture is also present, seen – for instance – in studio houses such as Sverre Fehn's Villa Holme (1998; see p. 152) in Norway, sculptor Ásmundur Sveinsson's magical home in Reykjavík (1942/1959; see p. 82) and, more recently, Studio Bua's Artist's Barn House (2021; see p. 286), also in Iceland.

Another fascinating thread to follow is the relationship between Nordic architecture and Japanese design and interiors. This can be seen in the work of mid-century masters such as Finn Juhl and Jakob Halldor Gunnløgsson, who recognized common cause in a shared focus on craft and organic materiality, as well as a fascination with inside–outside connectivity between the private realm and garden rooms. More recently, these passions are apparent in the work of contemporary Nordic architects such as Pálmar Kristmundsson in Iceland or Knut Hjeltnes in Norway, both of whom have spent time in Japan.

Returning to Sverre Fehn, he spoke about not only the importance of reading the language of the landscape but also the essential need to obtain a human scale in architecture. Along with many of the ideals outlined above, it is this innate respect for scale and proportion that lies at the heart of the Nordic home. These are houses that gently seek an accommodation with their surroundings while respecting each and every setting rather than making an imposition or a statement. But they are also buildings of warmth and welcome, where rooms and spaces are carefully designed around the needs of their inhabitants, as well as their dreams and desires. In this and many other respects, the iconic Nordic house offers an example to us all.

Lilla Hyttnäs

A curated combination of art and design

Carl & Karin Larsson

Sundborn
Sweden

1889/1900/1912

The dining room sits in the original part of the cottage and features crafted interiors with designs throughout by both Carl and Karin Larsson, including bespoke furniture and textiles. The 'cactus lampshades' over the table, also designed by the Larssons were added in 1903 after a hydroelectric plant was built nearby.

'My art is just like my home,' Carl Larsson once wrote. 'No fancy furniture fits there.... It is simple but harmonious, straightforward.'[1] Over time, Larsson's art and the home that he created with his wife, textile designer Karin Larsson, fused together to become part of a broader philosophy that referenced the Swedish vernacular, the Arts & Crafts movement and early modernism. It was an outlook on design that was unique, endearing and romantic, celebrated most famously in Carl Larsson's landmark book, *Ett Hem*, or *At Home*, originally published in 1899 and one of the first illustrated lifestyle titles. It helped to make the Larssons and Lilla Hyttnäs (Little Cabin), as their house was called, famous around the world.

Carl Larsson came from a poor Stockholm family, but his artistic talents were spotted at a young age and nurtured at the Royal Swedish Academy of Fine Arts. He first met Karin Bergöö at a Scandinavian artists' colony near Paris, with the couple soon discovering many shared interests as well as enjoying a broad frame of reference. They settled back in Stockholm but were then gifted a small cottage, Lilla Hyttnäs, by Karin's father, which had previously been used by his sisters but had just become vacant. Situated in the small and picturesque town of Sundborn, not far from the city of Falun, the Larssons initially used the cottage as a summer residence but, from 1889 onwards, it became their principal residence and workplace, as well as serving as the focal point of their family life.

Over the following years, the house began to grow, along with the family – the Larssons had eight children between 1884 and 1900. Initially, the couple remodelled the interiors of the existing cottage, including the dining room and drawing room, while adding spaces such as 'the workshop', which provided Carl with his first bespoke studio at Lilla Hyttnäs. The house itself also became a canvas for the Larssons, with Carl painting family portraits on door panels and adding decorative motifs to the surfaces of furniture and other integrated elements, while Karin designed most of the textiles. In this way, the colourful and multilayered interiors were a collaboration that developed over the years, along with the gradual evolution of the garden and fresh-air spaces.

Importantly, many of the portraits and motifs woven into the interiors referred back to the family itself, as seen in Carl's paintings of the children or Karin, who appears on the sliding door between the workshop and the central hallway. Antique furniture and Gustavian pieces feature prominently but were generally decorated or adapted by the Larssons. They also introduced custom pieces of their own design, including shades for the new electric lighting that was brought to the village in the form of a hydroelectric station in 1903. Salvaged items, such as the elegant eighteenth-century tiled stove in the drawing room, were also threaded into the mix.

While Carl was a masterful portrait painter, his work also encompassed interiors and landscapes, as well as monumental pieces and murals for installation in both public and private buildings, including schools and museums. For these commissions in particular, he needed more space, so at the turn of the century he designed and built a much larger art studio alongside the house. Completed at the end of 1899 and used from 1900 onwards, this is one of the most modern and innovative parts of Lilla Hyttnäs, providing a 'great room' in the Arts & Crafts style with high ceilings, open volumes and an integrated seating area around the fireplace. Here, especially, the interiors became a gallery, punctuated by his paintings, with the walls populated with a fresco replicated at the Norra Latin grammar school in Stockholm. Later, Carl extended the windows to the southern side of the studio to improve the quality of light, while also creating a direct link back to the house down a long hallway to the north, which provided extra hanging space for his paintings.

One of the last additions to Lilla Hyttnäs was the 'miner's cottage', which sits alongside the studio and was completed in 1912, just seven years before Carl's death. The cottage was created around eighteenth-century painted wall panels and ceilings rescued by the Larssons from a house near Falun that was due to be demolished. It was sometimes used as a summer bedroom by the Larssons themselves but also as a spacious and inviting guest room.

Now cared for by a family foundation and open to the public, Lilla Hyttnås retains the unique sense of character, personality and warmth that helped to make the house and its occupants renowned. Like the Bloomsbury Group's Charleston in East Sussex, England, it is a multilayered home that is an artwork in itself and one that evolved little by little and quite organically over time. It remains a key reference point in the world of interiors and residential design, as well as an essential exemplar in the development of the Scandinavian home.

Below A view of the garden room, or 'atrium', looking back to the dining room. The antique tiled stove was added by Carl Larsson, who also painted the ceiling patterns.

Left Every panel, window frame and surface in the house serves as a canvas for colour or pattern, as seen in Carl Larsson's bedroom, where the geometric pattern of the stained glass adds further interest.

Below The guest bedroom, or 'old room', features a box bed with doors inscribed with the names of visiting friends. The Larssons also added a motto on the ceiling with the words 'the truly old is only that which is eternally young'.

Above Carl Larsson's studio of 1900 is a generously scaled and modern space, with its high ceilings and bank of windows drawing in natural light. The rocking chair was designed by Karin Larsson while the eastern wall is covered in the 'draft' of a mural by Carl Larsson for the Norra Latin school in Stockholm.

Above The garden room is one of the most romantic and celebrated spaces at Lilla Hyttnäs and featured prominently in *Ett Hem*. The white furniture here once belonged to Karin Larsson's aunt.

Below Karin Larsson's bedroom was also where the children slept, in cots, when they were small. The room has an antique tiled stove, and Karin designed the 'rose of love' tapestry that hangs at the doorway to her husband's bedroom alongside.

Opposite The central hallway of Lilla Hyttnäs connects with many of the key spaces in the cottage, including the dining room and 'the workshop', which served as Carl Larsson's original studio and features his portrait of Karin Larsson on the doorway.

Hvitträsk

The threshold of modern living

Sitting on a hillside, looking out over the waters of Lake Vitträsk to the west of Helsinki, Eliel Saarinen's Finnish family home offers an extraordinary and original fusion of ideas. Hvitträsk stands on the cusp of tradition and modernity, combining elements of the vernacular with the Finnish National Romantic style as well as the Arts & Crafts style and more ornate Art Nouveau–inspired ingredients. The combined residence and architectural studio collectively known as Hvitträsk is unique in itself, possessing something of a fairy-tale quality enhanced by its sublime rural surroundings.

The house was born when Saarinen's career was flourishing. Having studied both art and architecture in Helsinki, Saarinen joined forces with colleagues Herman Gesellius and Armas Lindgren. During the first decade of the twentieth century, their practice won several major commissions, including the majestic Helsinki Central Railway Station (1906) and the National Museum of Finland (1910). Such success encouraged the partners to invest in a parcel of land at Lake Vitträsk, which is now around a thirty-minute drive from the city.

Initially, the property and its spacious architectural studio were shared by Saarinen, Gesellius and Lindgren. Saarinen and his first wife, Mathilda, moved into the south wing, Lindgren moved into the north wing (which was later destroyed in a fire and had to be rebuilt) and Gesellius moved into the Little Villa, sitting within the extensive gardens and grounds of the property. Over the following few years, there were many complications and dramatic changes, which saw Saarinen and Mathilda separating, and the architect later marrying Gesellius's sister, Loja, a textile designer. The couple had two children, Eero and Pipsan, both of whom would eventually become successful designers in their own right. The Lindgrens decided to move back to Helsinki in 1905, while Gesellius and Mathilda married and moved into the north wing.

'And so Hvitträsk was our home, in the full sense of the term,' said Eliel. 'It was where Pipsan and Eero grew up, and Loja and I came to know the feeling of spiritual affinity that I believe is the result of love.'[1] The south wing was the heart of the home, combining architecture, interiors, furniture and lighting within a total work of art, which also featured textiles and other designs by Loja as well as many designs by her husband.

The two most striking spaces in the house are the main living room and the dining room alongside it. The living room has the space, volume and openness of a great hall, with a drum-like tiled fireplace in one corner and oak furniture throughout, designed by Eliel and made by the Boman joinery in Turku. This elegant and spacious room, well suited to entertaining, offers a choice of seating zones, while the main staircase – where vivid blue walls contrast with crafted timber – climbs one wall, leading up towards the family's private realm.

The vaulted dining room and lounge alongside offer a more intimate and ornate space, with a seating area by the fireplace to one side and the dining area itself to the other. The banquette by the fireplace is softened by Saarinen's 'fairy-tale rug', another bespoke design representing scenes from the lives of the family, while the ceiling and the summit of the fireplace are enriched by decorative frescoes by the artist and neighbour Väinö Blomstedt. The stained-glass window next to the dining table, by Olga Gummerus-Ehrström, offers a striking focal point for this part of the room.

Upstairs, the family bedrooms and bathrooms have a lighter quality while also possessing a more modern aesthetic in terms of their relative restraint and simplicity, as well as the use of colour and light. Here, again, much of the furniture is by Saarinen, and many of these spaces offer a more vivid sense of connection with open views across the lake.

Alongside the south wing, the architectural studio is one of the most engaging spaces at Hvitträsk. It was originally shared by all three partners in the practice, yet with the departure of Lindgren and then the early death of Gesellius in 1916, the studio was left in Saarinen's hands alone. With its high ceilings and banks of windows facing the lake, it is a dramatic, open room, with space enough for a collection of drafting tables. There is a fireplace bordered with seating at the far end,

The design studio, with its views of Lake Vitträsk, was originally shared by Saarinen and his partners Armas Lindgren and Herman Gesellius. By 1916, the studio was being used solely by Saarinen and his design team. The plaster relief, by family friend Géza Maróti, is entitled *The Angel of Resurrection*.

Eliel Saarinen

Kirkkonummi
Finland

1903

where a large plaster relief entitled *The Angel of Resurrection*, by Géza Maróti, stands out, while a library and study, along with an inglenook fireplace, are situated at the point where the studio meets the house itself.

During the early 1920s, the Saarinens emigrated to the United States, where Eliel embarked on a second career, which famously included the design of many elements of the Cranbrook Academy of Art in Michigan, where he also served as president. Here, the Saarinens created a second extraordinary family home on the campus,[2] yet Hvitträsk continued to be their second home and summer house all the way through to 1949. Fully restored and well tended for, Hvitträsk, the Saarinens' home by the lake, is now open to the public.

Right The pivotal great room, or 'tupa', features a choice of spaces, including a dining area by the window (right) and a library, hidden by a protective curtain. The oak furniture here was designed by Saarinen and made by artisans in Turku, while the tiled fireplace (above) was also a bespoke design by the architect.

Right This house of many parts sits upon the bluff of a hillside, where it enjoys views across the lake and the surrounding landscape within this quiet, bucolic setting.

Below A detail of the studio, including the library created by Saarinen in 1916, and a desk designed by the architect and made by the Borman workshop in Turku (left). The main entrance to the house leads into a modestly scaled reception room with banquette seating and a welcoming fireplace (right).

Opposite With its vaulted ceilings, fireplace and engaging atmosphere, the formal dining room – or 'ruokasali' – is a room well suited to evening entertaining. As well as the dining table at one end, there is a substantial fitted couch with a 'ryijy' rug designed by Saarinen in 1914 with scenes of family life.

Left and below The principal bedroom and adjoining breakfast room, or morning salon, feature furniture by Saarinen throughout. The striking tiled stove in the bedroom has ornate copper stove doors designed by artist Eric O.W. Ehrström.

Below left The spacious children's playroom sits alongside Eero and Pipsan's bedroom, with both spaces enjoying elevated views of Lake Vitträsk. The fresco above the fireplace was designed by Väinö Blomstedt, while the furniture is by Saarinen.

Above The principal bathroom offers a re-creation of how the space would have been arranged and presented in 1910, complete with a stove boiler providing running hot water for the bathtub.

Villa Snellman

A marriage of modernity and tradition

Erik Gunnar Asplund

Djursholm
Sweden

1918

The great hall sits at the heart of the ground-floor plan, connecting with the dining room, living room, entrance hall and staircase. It is also a warm and welcoming space in its own right, with its sculptural stove coated in emerald tiles, and timber floors and ceilings.

As World War I came to an end, Swedish architect Erik Gunnar Asplund celebrated a landmark year. The pioneering modernist married his first wife in 1918 while also winning the competition to design one of the most important commissions of his career. This was Stockholm Public Library, completed in 1928, which brilliantly encapsulated the convergence of classicism and modernism within a single building. The crowning glory of the library is its extraordinary central rotunda, holding the circular reading room, which was set within an otherwise rectangular building lifted further by the striking geometric rhythm of the fenestration and detailing across its neatly ordered elevations.

More than this, 1918 also saw work finally getting underway on Asplund's Woodland Crematorium project for Stockholm City Council (designed in conjunction with his colleague Sigurd Lewerentz) and the completion of his most influential residential commission, Villa Snellman. Situated in the desirable neighbourhood of Djursholm, to the northeast of Stockholm, Villa Snellman also marries tradition and modernity to great effect. This highly original home references classicism and romanticism, yet is – at the same time – a modern house, rich in spatial shifts, illusions and surprises.

The residence was commissioned by a banker, who asked for a substantial, bespoke home for himself and his family, set in a generous garden. Asplund placed the villa on the gently sloping site with its two main storeys supplemented by an extensive basement, primarily for storage and services, as well as a large attic space. The intention was to build the house in stone, but limits to the budget meant that the house was ultimately constructed out of timber. Even so, the timber has been plastered and finished in such a way that visitors might imagine that stone or brick lies at the heart of the structure.

With the exterior painted a soft, soothing grey-white tone, the house has an imposing sense of height and grandeur as it sits within the garden, surrounded by mature trees. Yet the rectangular outline is subverted in a number of ways, which include a single-storey outrigger to one side, set at a slightly indented angle to the main body of the building rather than being placed at a true right angle. This additional element, holding the kitchen and other service spaces, helps to lighten and define the entrance courtyard, steering arrivals towards the threshold, where a projecting canopy shelters the front door.

Stepping inside, these subtle subversions continue. One wall of the entrance hallway is slightly tapered, leading guests quite naturally towards a more spacious great hall, which connects with the dining room and sitting room on either side of it, but is also an inviting room in its own right, with a striking stove coated in emerald tiles standing in one corner. This pivotal space also leads to the principal staircase, in one corner of the building, complemented by a secondary service stairway at the opposite end of the house.

Upstairs, again, there are modest but significant adjustments to an otherwise rectangular floor plan. The main landing, which runs almost the full length of the house, is also gently tapered, shifting the sense of perspective and creating the illusion of greater depth and extended space. As well as the family bedrooms and bathrooms, the upper storey holds a welcoming, cocoon-like circular salon with timber-panelled walls and a tiled stove. The ceiling height here is significantly higher than the spaces around it, an ambition that Asplund achieved by stealing space from the attic above. The high ceilings also offer the opportunity for an additional crescent-shaped clerestory, or fan window, placed above the rectangular aperture below. Such eccentricities add character to the layered interiors of the villa and while the round salon may not have the scale and grandeur of the circular reading room at the Public Library, the juxtaposition of geometrical forms here does offer a quiet echo of Asplund's masterpiece.

Still privately owned, the villa has been well cared for and carefully updated, with, for example, an upgraded kitchen with contemporary appliances. Many original features remain, including the tiled stoves, while a number of pieces of furniture designed by Asplund have been introduced, including his GA-2 chairs on the landing with their distinctive tubular steel legs.

The crisply rendered villa sits within a generous garden in the desirable suburb of Djursholm. The gentle slope of the site created the opportunity for a substantial basement level, while the pitched roof shelters a spacious attic.

Left The characterful double doorway of the main entrance, topped by a protective canopy, stands out against the soft, grey walls, as do other modest, decorative flourishes.

Opposite The tiled stoves, including the striking example in the great hall, are original to the house and fuse modern lines with traditional features.

Below The cabinet and matching furniture in the dining room date from the 1930s and were produced by Uppsala Möblerings.

Right The kitchen has been sensitively upgraded for modern use while preserving original ingredients.

Opposite The ground-floor sitting room, alongside the great hall, also features an original tiled stove, with its circular design framed by a niche next to the doorway.

Above The GA-1 Chair in the entrance hall was designed by Asplund during the 1930s.

Above right The principal bedroom on the upper floor also features a tiled stove.

Opposite The curvaceous, wooden-panelled salon offers a more intimate retreat, while the circular room contrasts with the linear outline of the house itself and the majority of its spaces.

Villa Carlsten

Characterful coastal escapism

Today, Josef Frank is best known for his exuberant textile designs and his extensive collections of furniture created for the Swedish design house Svenskt Tenn. Frank became closely associated with the company after meeting its founder, Estrid Ericson, in the early 1930s, following his decision to emigrate from Austria to Sweden, where he settled with his Scandinavian wife and eventually became a Swedish citizen. Many of Frank's most famous and enduring designs date from the 1940s and 1950s, with their joyful yet decidedly modern aesthetic helping to define mid-century Nordic interiors.

Yet Frank was also a much-respected architect, with many of his key architectural commissions dating from the 1920s and early 1930s when he was working between Austria and Sweden. Five of his houses are located in the southern Swedish resort town of Falsterbo, along the shores of the Øresund Strait, which became fashionable during the inter-war period, with architects such as Sigurd Lewerentz also designing homes here.

Frank and his wife, Anna Sebenius, began visiting Falsterbo regularly in the 1920s while they were still living in Vienna, where his atelier and a home-furnishing business called Haus & Garten were based. Over time Frank got to know the coastal town very well, which is just along the coast from Malmö, and in 1924 he was asked to design a house for his brother-in-law and his wife, Axel and Signhild Claësen. Their summer house, Villa Claësen, was the first of a handful of vacation villas that Frank designed in Falsterbo over the following years, as family connections and friendships led to other new projects.

One of the smallest but most engaging of these projects was Villa Carlsten. This summer residence was commissioned by Signe and Allan Carlsten, with the site a small distance from the coastline and sitting within a generously sized garden. Here, Frank designed a timber-framed, two-storey building that was intended to make the most of the setting, with architectural elements including integrated balconies and outdoor spaces.

The ground floor is largely devoted to a welcoming great room, but one which includes various shifts in ceiling height, volume and scale. The front door opens on to a small vestibule that leads directly into this living room, which is filled with sunlight from its well-proportioned windows and tied together by its wooden floors, white walls and woodwork, including timber ceilings. Although the space is essentially open plan, Frank created a series of distinct zones. Two outriggers offer a choice of dining or breakfast nooks, while a lounge area with a comfortable Svenskt Tenn sofa sits to one side, next to the doorway leading through to the kitchen, pantry and back door.

The staircase to the upper floor wraps around and behind the elegant fireplace in the living room, leading upwards to the two principal bedrooms. These, in turn, revolve around a substantial landing, which also offers an additional lounge, while each of the two private retreats benefits from French windows leading out to the balconies placed on the rooftops of the outriggers below. These balconies look out on the open garden and originally – before other houses were built in the neighbourhood – offered views of the coast itself.

Not long after the house was completed, in 1927, the Carlstens realized that they had underestimated their own needs and asked Frank to modestly extend the main house. Later still, a pavilion was added to one side, holding a family-sized bathroom, utility room and two more bedrooms. There is also a pergola and outdoor seating areas, which include furniture designed by Frank himself.

Villa Carlsten is now owned and cared for by the Kjell and Märta Beijer Foundation, which owns Svenskt Tenn. The house has been carefully restored and layered with Frank's furniture and textiles. Conservation architect Mikael Bergquist responded to former alterations to the kitchen, pantry and small maid's room, where partition walls had already been removed, by creating a more substantial and spacious kitchen and breakfast area with sympathetic fittings and furnishings throughout.

For Frank, the Falsterbo sequence of villas, which took him through to the early 1930s and the point where he settled in Sweden,

The ground floor of the house is largely consumed by a spacious, multifaceted living room, where the bay windows help to define spaces for relaxing or dining with views over the garden.

Villa Carlsten

Left and below Fitted benches sit around the dining table within the projecting bay that frames the principal dining area in the living room (left). The fireplace is opposite, with the stairs to the upper floor curling around it (below).

Opposite The kitchen features furniture by Frank, while the placemats depict patterns by Frank for Svenskt Tenn. The modern kitchen units were designed by Mikael Bergquist.

provided one of the most significant elements of his architectural portfolio. They offered an opportunity to create a set of homes that were, in their own way, modernist in their design philosophy yet also characterful, relaxed and engaging, in keeping with the resort setting. In this respect, they compare with lots of Frank's most famous designs for Svenskt Tenn, many of which have been reissued over recent years and remain in production.

Below Upstairs there are two bedrooms with balconies overlooking the garden. The textiles for the curtains and desk chair are by Frank for Svenskt Tenn.

Opposite With Villa Carlsten, Frank has taken the idea of a neat modernist cube and added character, subtlety and interest with its outriggers and balconies, while introducing a similar sense of delight to the spaces within.

Rothenborg House

Innovative Danish modernism

With its backdrop of mature trees, the crisp, modern outline of the house stands out in its garden setting. Ribbon windows, decks and terraces all help to dissolve boundaries between outside and in.

The resulting house is a highly sophisticated and rounded home, particularly for a young architect who had not even reached his thirtieth birthday.

The coastal community of Klampenborg, to the north of Copenhagen, played a key part in the evolution of Arne Jacobsen's career during the 1930s. Sitting on the main railway line running from Copenhagen to Helsingør, Klampenborg became an enticing destination from the late nineteenth century onwards. Easy links back to the city made this a desirable neighbourhood for those who wanted to live by the beach but regularly commuted to the city, while visitors coming the other way turned Klampenborg into one of Denmark's most popular coastal resorts in the early decades of the twentieth century.

Jacobsen, who only graduated from the Royal Danish Academy of Fine Arts in 1927, managed to secure a handful of key commissions in and around Klampenborg during the early years of his practice. These included the Bellevue sea bath project of 1932, right on the shore, which encompassed everything from Jacobsen's distinctive watchtowers for the lifeguards to kiosks, changing cabins and even the design of the season tickets. Beyond this, Jacobsen secured a handful of other commissions little more than a stone's throw away, including the Bellavista apartment complex (1934), the Bellevue Theatre (1936) and also the pioneering Skovshoved filling station (1936) on the main road, which is still in use.

There were also a number of important private family houses here, as well as in neighbouring Charlottenlund, including his own home (1929) and the Rothenborg House of 1931. These early houses suggest the influence of Jacobsen's travels in Germany and Europe during the 1920s and his embrace of early modernism, as reflected in the functionalist, flat-roofed, cubist compositions coated in white stucco.

The Rothenborg House was commissioned by the lawyer Max Rothenborg and his wife, who shared an interest in modern architecture and interiors. They asked Jacobsen to design a spacious villa in the modernist style, while granting him a considerable degree of trust and the freedom to further his ideas.

The resulting house is a highly sophisticated and rounded home, particularly for a young architect who had not even reached his thirtieth birthday. Sitting in a generous and secluded garden, bordered by trees, Jacobsen created a building in three parts, built of brick but coated in smooth render and painted white. The U-shaped plan, which wraps around the entrance court, includes a garage to one side and a two-storey element to the other, holding the kitchen and maid's quarters on the ground level with bedrooms and bathrooms above.

The central section of the house, which is largely single storey, holds the main entrance, the key living spaces and also the primary suite, effectively offering a self-contained home within a home. Services are largely held in a hidden basement, further liberating this pivotal part of the villa, where the living spaces are generously scaled. The sitting room and the adjoining dining room, in particular, are welcoming spaces, which are enriched by ribbon windows framing views of the garden while also offering connections to a substantial terrace, complete with an outdoor fireplace.

Jacobsen provided the Rothenborgs with a choice of outdoor rooms and fresh-air spaces, including a roof terrace perched on top of one of the lower portions of the building and accessed via the two-storey wing. As with so many of his other projects, Jacobsen was involved not only with the architecture, but also with the landscaping, interiors and detailing. Many original elements, such as the fireplaces, have been protected and preserved during the recent restoration and upgrade of the house, which is still privately owned. During the post-war period, Jacobsen built a second home for himself nearby, also located in Klampenborg.

Increasingly, during the 1950s and 1960s Jacobsen became an influential polymath, whose work embraced a rich range of typologies. His landmark mid-century projects include the SAS Royal Hotel in Copenhagen of 1960, where his work encompassed not only the architecture of the iconic building but also the interiors, the lighting, the cutlery and much more besides. Jacobsen's famous Egg and Swan chairs were originally designed for the SAS project. Later, in his design for St Catherine's College at the University of Oxford, his remit even extended to the choice of fish for the ornamental ponds within the elegantly landscaped grounds.

Below The main entrance to the central part of the house is framed by the two-storey block to the right and garaging to the left; the main living spaces sit at the heart of the plan.

Left and below The living room leads out to a substantial sequence of terraces at the rear of the house, including an outdoor living room arranged around a fireplace and defined by the curving garden wall.

Below and opposite
The rear terraces enhance the overall sense of space, offering semi-sheltered outdoor rooms with a natural sense of connection to the living spaces within, where natural light is maximized by the generosity of the glazing and the pale colour palette throughout.

Villa Mairea

A pioneering rural retreat

Alvar Aalto's Villa Mairea offers the most rounded, accomplished, luxurious and original single-family home designed by Finland's leading modernist architect. The house, set within the forests of Noormarkku in the west of the country, provided an opportunity for experimentation within an engaging rural setting, which Aalto fully embraced. Along with the architect's own homes in Helsinki and Muuratsalo, Villa Mairea offered a golden opportunity for fresh thinking, with Aalto actively encouraged and pushed onwards by his close friends and colleagues, Maire and Harry Gullichsen, who commissioned the extraordinary residence. Maire was the daughter of Finnish industrialist Valter Ahlström, who had built up a vast timber and forestry business that was run by Harry following the untimely death of her father.

'We told him that he should regard it as an experimental house,' said Maire, after whom the house is named. 'If it didn't work out, we wouldn't blame him for it. Every detail was discussed.'[1] The Gullichsens shared many of Aalto's ideals as well as the wish to create a truly exemplary home, with a resonance that would extend well beyond their own needs and wishes. By the time that Villa Mairea was born, Alvar and Aino Aalto had known the Gullichsens for some years.

As well as believing in the modernist ideal that good design could make the world a better place, the Gullichsens shared a love of modern art, architecture and culture. In 1935, Maire co-founded the furniture company Artek with the Aaltos and Nils-Gustav Hahl, with the company going on to produce many of Alvar Aalto's designs. The Ahlström company, under Harry Gullichsen's leadership, commissioned Aalto to work on a number of projects, while the couple also asked him to design the interiors of their flat in Helsinki, as well as their family escape in Noormarkku, set among the Ahlström woodlands.

The natural setting within the forest was to play a key part in the evolution of Villa Mairea, one of Alvar Aalto's most organic projects. It sits within a clearing among the trees, and the use of a predominantly natural palette of materials, including timber cladding, ties the building to the landscape. More than this, Aalto sought to bring the surroundings into the two-storey house through multiple means. This process begins with the extended porch over the front door, where the sinuous canopy is held by a sequence of slim, supporting columns that echo the towering trees all around. This idea continues inside the home, where the entrance hallway is bordered with similar supports, as is the feature staircase, and steel columns within the open-plan living room are wrapped in raffia. Pine, hornbeam and teak are used extensively within the beautifully crafted interiors, along with ceramic floor tiles, slate and brickwork, which is often painted white. Extensive fenestration also draws in the forest and garden, while integrated planters and a winter garden enhance the sensation of being immersed in the natural world.

The programme for the villa itself evolved a number of times, in close consultation with the Gullichsens. The idea of a welcoming great room developed over many plans and sketches, with the original aim of a separate gallery and living space dropped in favour of a generously scaled focal point that served not only as a sitting room but also as a music room, a gallery and more, tied together by the red tiled floor and slatted timber ceilings. Harry Gullichsen, however, did insist on a separate library/study to one side, where he could work and hold meetings. The winter garden and also the dining room are spaces in their own right, with the kitchen and service areas positioned close by, forming part of an L-shaped plan that wraps around a semi-sheltered garden with its kidney-shaped swimming pool. Upstairs, there are family bedrooms and guest accommodation, while Maire was provided with an elegant corner studio, with high ceilings and curvaceous walls.

Importantly, Aalto was characteristically involved in almost every aspect of the design of the villa, from the architecture to the landscaping and the interiors. This included details such as the door handles, shelving and railings, as well as much of the furniture, along with work by Aino, with some of these pieces later produced by Artek. In this way, Villa Mairea could be seen, like Aalto's own homes,

The carefully curated palette of materials in the pivotal great room, with its tiled floors and wooden ceilings, reinforces the organic warmth of the architecture and interiors seen throughout Villa Mairea.

Alvar Aalto

Noormarkku
Finland

1939

Villa Mairea

as a total work of art. Yet the Gullichsens also provided an additional layer through their collection of modern paintings and other artworks, including pieces by Picasso, Juan Gris, Alexander Calder, Jean Arp and others.

The influence of Japanese design on Villa Mairea has been recognized by a number of commentators, while others have drawn comparisons with the organic homes designed by Frank Lloyd Wright. But this is not to detract from the originality of Villa Mairea, which has certainly attained iconic status as a key exemplar of twentieth-century residential architecture and design.

'The house was the product of a propitious set of circumstances and a happy combination of like-minded personalities,' suggests the owners' son, Kristian Gullichsen. 'The building bears witness to a creative interchange between architect and clients. All the evidence indicates that they egged each other on to ever more ambitious ideas as the work progressed. The final result clearly reflects the architect's reading of his clients' personalities: my mother's passionate interest in modern art, and my father's career in the forest industry. The Cubist form world dissolves into the symbols of the forest.'[2]

Opposite and above
The house engages with the surrounding forest, while also responding to it in the use of natural materials and ideas inspired by the woods, including the copse of slender, tree-like pillars supporting the entrance canopy. The naturalistic design of the gardens fits in with Aalto's organic approach.

Villa Mairea
AALTO Villa Mairea

Opposite and above
Wooden supports around the staircase and raffia-wrapped pillars in the great room are also suggestive of the surrounding forest, while the entrance hall can be seen a few steps down from the living room. Much of the furniture here was designed by Aalto, including the iconic tea trolley produced by Artek.

Left Integrated planters in a corner of the living room enhance the organic character of the interiors, while the greenery provides a connection with the gardens framed by the large picture windows.

Above and opposite The separate winter garden sits alongside the living room, offering a halfway point between inside and outside space, with its stone flag floors, planting throughout and doorway to the garden.

The influence of Japanese design on Villa Mairea has been recognized by a number of commentators, while others have drawn comparisons with the organic homes designed by Frank Lloyd Wright.

Left The upstairs studio is situated next to the primary suite, with a mezzanine level leading out to one of a choice of balconies, decks and terraces overlooking the surrounding landscape.

Above As well as Maire Gullichsen's studio (left), the principal suite and guest accommodation, the upper storey holds the children's bedrooms and a substantial playroom, complete with swing and play equipment (right).

Villa Stenersen

A living landmark on an Oslo hillside

Arne Korsmo

Oslo
Norway

1939

The house has been pushed gently into the hillside, offering an integrated, semicircular garage at lower-ground level with three storeys of living space above, looking out over the gardens and the city beyond.

The entrepreneurial Rolf Stenersen nurtured many interests. He was a gifted economist and financier who made his fortune trading in stocks and shares during the 1920s and married Inger Johanne Martinsen, better known as Annie, in 1924. They had two children while also pursuing a passion for modern art, which carried through Stenersen's life, becoming increasingly important over subsequent decades. Stenersen became, in particular, an avid collector of Norwegian artist Edvard Munch's work, building one of the largest private collections of his paintings and getting to know him well over the years. Also respected as a talented writer, Stenersen produced a landmark biography of the artist, *Edvard Munch: Close-Up of a Genius*, first published in 1945 and reprinted many times. 'Visual stimulation has meant so much to me,' said Stenersen. 'Everything I know, everything I've learned, everything good has come to me through sight. When I see something beautiful, I have an almost religious experience. I'm filled with reverence, gratitude and joy at being able to observe and experience it.'[1]

This love of the visual arts also extended to modern architecture. During the mid-1930s Stenersen approached the pioneering Norwegian modernist architect Arne Korsmo and commissioned him to design a new house within the leafy neighbourhood of Borgen to the northwest of Oslo's city centre. The house needed to be spacious enough to accommodate the young family and to provide spaces suited to entertaining and for appreciating the growing collection of paintings and sculptures.

Korsmo developed an innovative design for a four-storey building, using a concrete framework and expanses of glass, while pushing the house sideways into the hillside site. This allowed for the provision of an integrated, crescent-shaped garage at lower-ground level, accessed from the driveway, as well as basement service spaces. Steps lead up to the main entrance and the reception rooms and salons on the raised ground floor, while an outdoor spiral staircase connects directly with the piano nobile above.

The piano nobile offers an extraordinary open-plan living space that soon became the heart of the house. Here, Korsmo created a spacious great room running the entire length of the building with a wall of glass bricks and picture windows looking out onto the gardens and framing views across the city beyond. A dining area was positioned at one end, with easy access to the kitchen situated towards the rear of the building, while the rest of the room was devoted to a choice of seating areas around a feature fireplace. Stenersen's private study and writing room was also located on this principal level, complete with a large picture window to one side looking out onto the trees.

The top floor was devoted to the family bedrooms, which also enjoy open vistas and benefit from an integrated balcony running the length of the front elevation, which is remarkable for its rhythmic geometry. At the same time, the house was designed to be efficient and practical, with the main staircase – topped by a skylight made up of coloured glass discs – neatly tying the different levels together, while bathrooms and service spaces are pushed to the back of the house on each storey. Functional spaces, such as the primary bathroom, are also striking for their sophistication, with elegant tilework and a vivid use of colour, which was also employed to great effect in other spaces, such as the ground-floor salon and bar.

Artworks were displayed throughout, including many pieces by Edvard Munch, while sculptures punctuate the winding stairway. During the 1970s, towards the end of his life, Stenersen decided to donate his extensive art collection to the cities of Bergen and Oslo, with many of the Munch artworks now held by the eponymous art museum on the waterfront dedicated to the painter's portfolio. Stenersen also gifted the house to the Norwegian state, with the idea that it might be used by key dignitaries, although ultimately just one prime minister, Odvar Nordli, decided to live at Villa Stenersen. The house is now looked after by the National Museum of Norway, which has restored the building as well as opening it to the public.

Arne Korsmo's career continued into the mid-century period, with the architect widely regarded as one of the most influential Scandinavian modernists. Korsmo designed an innovative Oslo home for himself, completed in 1955, alongside two matching homes on the northern edge of the city. Notably, Korsmo was a friend and mentor to Sverre Fehn (see p. 152), who eventually chose to live in an Oslo home, Villa Damman, originally designed by Korsmo in the 1930s and subsequently updated by Fehn himself.

Below and right
The interiors contrast pale floors and ceilings with bursts of colour, as seen in the garden room alongside the main entrance on the ground floor. Korsmo used mustard yellow for the end wall and the bespoke bar in the corner next to it.

Left The house offers a vivid sense of connectivity between inside and out, as seen in the garden room where a wall of floor-to-ceiling glass frames views of the terrace and gardens.

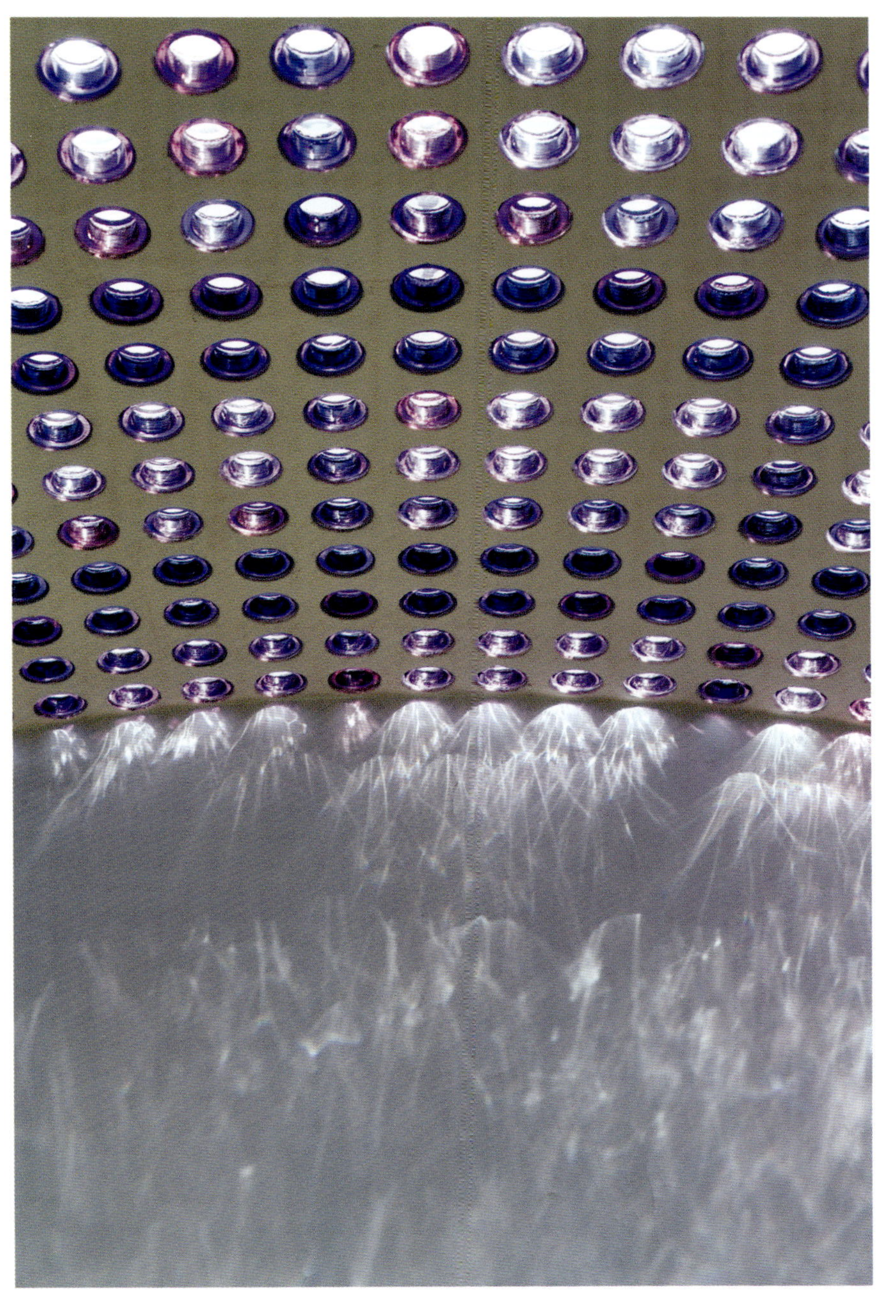

Left and above A skylight made up of coloured, circular glass discs brings light into the stairwell, which is used not only for circulation and as a source of light, but also for the display of art and sculpture.

Opposite Rolf Stenersen's private study is situated at mid-level, alongside the living room, and includes bespoke shelving and storage units as well as a desk facing a large picture window on the side elevation of the house.

Above The substantial piano nobile at mid-level is devoted to a spacious living room running the entire length of the house. Windows are framed by walls of glass bricks, while other walls are dedicated to the display of art.

Juhl House

At home with the Danish style

The house that architect and furniture designer Finn Juhl designed for himself is, at one and the same time, a home, a design studio and a showcase for many of his best-known pieces. Sitting in a generous garden in the village of Ordrup, alongside Charlottenlund to the north of Copenhagen, the house offers one of the fullest and most cohesive expressions of Juhl's prolific creative output, fusing the many aspects of his work in the most personal manner, including architecture, interiors and furniture. It is also layered with art, sculpture and textiles by friends and associates, making it one of the most rounded and characterful expressions of the mid-century modern style in Denmark.

The house came relatively early in Juhl's long career when he was still married to his first wife and working in Vilhelm Lauritzen's architectural office. Yet just a few years after completing the house in 1942, Juhl had established his own atelier and was busy developing his furniture portfolio, as well as taking occasional architectural and interiors commissions. Although his design studio was in Copenhagen, the house also served as a second office, with the interiors slowly evolving over the decades as one new piece of furniture or painting after another made its presence felt.

Juhl acquired the parcel of land next to the mansion of Ordrupgaard (now an art museum) after the death of his father, a textile merchant, and the receipt of an inheritance in 1941. He designed an L-shaped building in the garden that was largely on one level (with the exception of a cellar) but also gently pushed into the sloping site, resulting in subtle changes of floor level. The house features a softly pitched tiled roofline and is rendered white, yet it is distinctly modern in other respects, with extensive banks of glass looking into the garden at key points, as well as a fluid and partially open-plan layout internally.

The house is accessed via an entrance vestibule and hallway that sits at the junction of the L-shaped plan and lightly separates the two distinct wings of the house. A modestly scaled office is positioned to one side of the vestibule, while the stairway down to the cellar sits opposite. Stepping into the hallway, reveals a wall of glass framing an open view of the adjoining terrace and the garden beyond. 'We wanted it rural and simple,' said Juhl of his house, 'a mixture of a summerhouse and a bit of legitimate elegance.'[1]

One wing of the house is devoted to a spacious lounge, in three distinct zones. There is a seating area around a fireplace and another arranged around an integrated banquette and a table by a corner window, yet a substantial portion of the room is allocated to Juhl's library, with its fitted bookshelves and banks of storage, as well as a work desk illuminated by another corner window. Wooden floors tie the wing together and the pitched ceiling enhances the sense of space. The room is, of course, populated with Juhl's own furniture designs, including his famous Poet Sofa, first designed in 1941, and his high-backed Chieftain Chair (1949), both positioned around the fireplace. Both of these iconic pieces, along with the majority of Juhl's early designs, were produced by Niels Vodder and characterized by their sinuous, sculptural forms and ergonomic quality.

From the central hallway a few steps lead up to the second wing, arranged at right angles to the first. This part of the house holds the kitchen, a dining room and then, beyond the bathroom and modest guest room, a substantial principal bedroom that also served as a private lounge. In the winter months, the fire was lit and the room functioned as a largely self-contained apartment, with a circular table for working and reading illuminated by a Poul Henningsen pendant light.

Here, again, the furniture is by Juhl, including the bed and the folding chest of drawers, which he initially designed as a glove cabinet for his second partner, Hanne Wilhelm Hansen, who joined him at the house in 1961. With just two bedrooms, as well as Juhl's flexible workspaces, the house is relatively modest in scale. Yet it is richly layered with furniture, books and art, with paintings by Vilhelm Lundstrøm, including a portrait of Hanne, as well as works by Richard Mortensen, Asger Jorn and Georges Braque.

The house was a constant presence in Juhl's life. In the 1950s, when Baker Furniture

The spacious living room occupies one wing of the house and serves as a lounge, library and study all in one. Among the many pieces of Juhl's own design within the room, one of the most familiar is his Chieftain Chair by the fireplace.

Finn Juhl

Ordrup
Denmark

1942

began marketing Juhl's furniture in the United States with great success, his work reached a wider audience than ever before. Juhl was also asked to design the interiors of the Trusteeship Council Chamber at the United Nations Headquarters in New York during the 1950s, and he won three gold medals for his furniture at the Milan Triennial of 1957. The house assumed even greater importance during the early 1960s, as Juhl gave up his Copenhagen studio to focus on working largely from home.

The garden, too, laid out by landscape architect Troels Erstad, was an important ingredient, with Juhl taking inspiration from, among other things, the respectful relationship between house and garden seen in Japan. The designer's home library still includes a selection of books on Japanese architecture and design. 'Our architecture's natural setting, with a garden area, is something we have learnt from the Japanese,' said Juhl, 'who are masters at incorporating their houses into beautiful open spaces.'[2]

The house is now open to the public, forming part of the Ordrupgaard Museum. A full-scale replica of the designer's residence has also been created in the city of Gifu in Japan, suggesting the continuing resonance of Juhl's work around the world as well as the intrinsic warmth, character and charm of his home.

Below Juhl's corner study in the main living room includes wall-mounted bookcases and storage units, a drawing-board table and an FJ46 desk chair (1946).

Opposite The corner seating area, also in the living-room wing, has a fitted sofa around a 1960s table, as well as a pair of FJ45 easy chairs (1945).

CRETE AND MYCENAE

Above The L-shaped house sits in a quiet garden, with a backdrop of trees beyond. The wing to the right holds the living room while the principal bedroom is at the other end of the house.

Above Juhl's celebrated Poet Sofa is next to the fireplace, while the painting by Vilhelm Lundstrøm is of the designer's partner, Hanne Wilhelm Hansen.

Above right The study zone of the living room includes a colourful set of filing shelves and integrated storage. Juhl also used a separate office alongside the central entrance hall.

Opposite The main entrance connects with a garden room at the centre of the plan, with fitted seating and planters that echo the greenery beyond the banks of glass.

Right The compact corner kitchen was ergonomically designed, with a wealth of fitted storage complemented by stainless-steel counters around the sink in front of the window.

Above During the colder winter months, Juhl retreated into the spacious primary bedroom, where there was a work/dining table, a lounge area and a library, holding part of his collection of literature and reference books on wall-mounted shelving.

Above Other furniture in the principal bedroom includes a bed designed by Juhl in 1961 and a set of FJ48 chairs around the circular table. The ceiling light is by Poul Henningsen.

Ásmundarsafn

The house of sculpture

Ásmundur Sveinsson & Einar Sveinsson

Reykjavík
Iceland

1942/1959

Ásmundur Sveinsson's distinctive house and studio is set in a generous garden, which is home to a number of his larger sculptures, including the troll-like *Giantess* of 1948

'If I'd never done any building, none of my large sculptures would exist – not one.'

The celebrated Icelandic sculptor Ásmundur Sveinsson recognized the close relationship between architecture and art. More than this, the two fields often overlapped and interconnected in Sveinsson's work, with his more monumental pieces of sculpture sometimes adopting an architectural quality, particularly his ironwork designs. Sveinsson's talents extended to the architecture and construction of his own houses and studios, seen most dramatically at Ásmundarsafn in Reykjavík, where he created a unique and highly individual home that served as a creative hub.

'If I'd never done any building, none of my large sculptures would exist – not one,' said Ásmundur Sveinsson. 'It's impossible to enlarge models except in good studios, bright and roomy, with high ceilings. Buildings like that don't exist here in this country. And no wonder; there are so few sculptors.'[1]

Sveinsson learnt many practical craft skills as a child, growing up on his parents' farm in the west of Iceland, where he was one of eleven siblings. Even at a young age, his imagination travelled far beyond his rural surroundings, as he nursed the dream of becoming an artist. The search for broader horizons and a rounded education took him first to Reykjavík, where he studied wood carving and draughtsmanship. Encouraged to pursue his talents, Sveinsson then left Iceland for a decade, studying and working in Copenhagen, Stockholm and Paris.

Eventually, in 1930, Sveinsson returned to Iceland and staged his first solo exhibition in his home country that same year. Just a few years later, in 1933, assisted by a grant from the Icelandic state, the sculptor designed and built his first home and home studio in Reykjavík on the central arterial thoroughfare, Freyjugata. Over the following years, both the scale and ambition of Sveinsson's sculptural portfolio evolved rapidly, drawing on Icelandic folklore and myth while also adopting a level of abstraction that placed him in the wider world of avant-garde modernism.

By the early 1940s, Sveinsson – and his work – had outgrown all available space at Freyjugata, and he began thinking about designing a new home and studio to be shared with his second wife, Ingrid. The sculptor settled on a garden site not far from Reykjavík's Botanical Gardens and Zoo, within a quiet residential neighbourhood. Ásmundarsafn evolved in three distinct phases, beginning with the house itself, topped by a domed gallery.

Like Sveinsson's art, the resulting home was highly individual. The building referenced Greek classicism, Egyptian monuments and Turkish architecture, yet was also, in its own way, distinctly modern. It resembles a temple, or perhaps an observatory, with its striking combination of the central dome and then two pyramidal forms to either side of the building, added in 1946, four years after the completion of the central section of the house. The unadorned, pale concrete surfaces and the rhythmic fenestration lend the building a suitably sculptural character and a marked sense of purity.

Later, as Sveinsson was experimenting with welded ironwork sculptures, as well as wood and stone, he decided to create a new studio to the rear of the house, assisted by Reykjavík's City Architect, Einar Sveinsson. Completed in 1959, the new studio was crescent-shaped and bathed in natural light from a combination of a large skylight and a clerestory window positioned around the curvaceous staircase situated at the junction of the two distinct parts of the building, as well as additional banks of glass within the outstretched wings of the studio space. Parts of this new addition, called 'The Shed', were double-height, allowing Ásmundur Sveinsson to work on much larger pieces.

'One might say that the construction work has done me considerable good,' said Sveinsson. 'In the meantime I've had a rest from my art, and that has increased my mental fecundity. It's hard for artists to work constantly on artistic creations without being repetitive. They need to renew themselves.'[2] Certainly, the completion of the new studio marked the beginning of another highly productive period, with Sveinsson's sculptures gaining international attention during the 1960s and 1970s. In 1960, he exhibited at the Venice Biennale for the first time and, in 1971, the National Gallery of Iceland staged a major retrospective exhibition.

Following the artist's death in 1982, Ásmundarsafn – or the Ásmundur Sveinsson Sculpture Museum, as it is also known – was opened to the public. He left his work to the city of Reykjavík, with many of his larger pieces exhibited in the grounds of the studio house. In this way, art and architecture continue to combine and enrich one another at one of the city's most unusual and iconic buildings.

The spacious studio-gallery, 'The Shed', was added in 1959 with the assistance of architect Einar Sveinsson. The double-height spaces are top-lit and capable of housing large-scale pieces of work.

Above The main entrance to the house is flanked by two Sveinsson sculptures, *The Gardener* and *The Weatherman*, both dating from 1934; the former was modelled on the sculptor's brother.

Right Like the temple-like exteriors, the interiors of the house and studio also explore unusual geometries, tricks of the eye, shifts in scale and spatial illusions within their complex, sculptural forms.

Above The crescent-shaped form and high roofline of 'The Shed', or studio, contrast with the original house. There is a gallery space upstairs in the central dome.

Utzon House

The new courtyard house

Jørn Utzon

Hellebæk
Denmark

1952/1959

The living room in the original part of the house sits alongside the tiled entrance hallway. The sliding doorway beyond the hall leads to a work studio and drafting room.

The house in the woods that architect Jørn Utzon created for himself and his family was designed in two distinct phases during the 1950s. The project began with a relatively compact two-bedroom building with a wall of glass facing the landscape within the woodland site close to the coastal town of Hellebæk. But, after the arrival of the Utzons' third child and his competition-winning entry for the iconic Sydney Opera House project, Utzon radically extended the house into a much more spacious courtyard home, united by a cohesive palette of brick and timber. In this respect, the house grew organically, evolving with the needs of the family while also forging a strong sense of connectivity with the surroundings and the natural world.

The son of a naval architect, Utzon grew up in Aalborg, but Hellebæk was always seen as a second home, given that the family kept a summer house nearby, which Utzon visited regularly as a child. Knowing the area well, Utzon and his wife decided to settle there after a period spent travelling in the United States and Mexico during the late 1940s.

'He felt very at home here and liked being in nature,' says his son, architect and artist Jan Utzon, who now lives in the house. 'Also, it's not too distant from Copenhagen and it only takes 45 minutes to the city, although he never actually had an office in Copenhagen. The office was in the town here, in Hellebæk, where he rented a floor in a warehouse that belonged to the local textile factory.'[1]

Although not far from Hellebæk and the coast, the site of the house has a bucolic, escapist character that comes from its setting within a quiet clearing in the woods. Working with a modest budget and in close cooperation with local craftsmen, Utzon initially designed a rectangular building that largely turned its back to the north – where the main entrance and garage were located – while opening up dramatically to the south, where the meadow slopes gently towards the trees. Utzon originally placed the children's bedroom at one end, the primary bedroom at the other, while the main living area was placed at the centre, with a compact kitchenette and a dining area to one side. Sliding doors were used to create a degree

The glass link connects the 'new' and old parts of the house while partly framing the resulting courtyard garden. Artworks are largely by Jørn's Utzon's son and owner of the house, architect Jan Utzon.

of flexibility within the layout, while terraces and outdoor rooms around the house add to the feeling of space.

'The partitions and doors consist of frames on which Oregon pine boards were mounted, so they all look alike,' said Jørn Utzon. 'Thus one avoids being restricted by the dimensions that a door actually has in a room. The walls are joined to the ceiling and floors with black-painted wooden moulding, so the walls can be moved and altered in size as needed in the future.'[2]

Similarly, Utzon incorporated an easily adaptable lighting system and introduced underfloor heating, which offered a uniform temperature and also helped to save space. The yellow brickwork was carefully crafted, both within and without, working in sympathy with the pale woodwork of the ceilings and joinery.

The 'constructive and functional approach combined with a sensitivity for light, shadow, colour and space, offers unlimited possibilities,' Utzon said of the first phase of the project. And, just a few years later, with his portfolio growing and the Sydney commission secured, the architect felt able to embark on the second phase, which involved adding another, longer rectangular structure behind the first, adopting similar principles and the same palette of materials. Here, Utzon created a more generously scaled family kitchen and dining room, while each of his three children was given a private space of their own in the bedroom wing, along with the provision of a new principal suite. A glass-sided link connected this new part of the house to the old, while the former garage was also upgraded and subsumed into the overall plan, resulting in a courtyard house.

The courtyard solution was ingenious, lending the enlarged house an almost seamless sense of unity while ensuring that every key room had a vivid connection either to the courtyard or to the surrounding terraces and gardens. Again, the internal space was maximized with, for example, a neat line of storage cupboards running down the northern wall of the hallway that gives access to the family bedrooms. At the same time, the enlarged house now provided adequate space for Utzon to work from home, as he wished, as well as using the office in town. The beauty of the courtyard layout was further explored with Utzon's Kingo Housing project at nearby Helsingør (1959), which the architect was working on at around the same time, as well as his Fredensborg Houses (1963).

Utzon and his family spent part of the 1960s in Australia while he worked on the Opera House, and later split their time between Denmark, Hawaii and Mallorca, where the architect famously designed another two private homes. Eventually, the Danish and the Mallorcan houses were divided among the three children, with Jan Utzon returning to the house in Hellebæk, which he has sensitively restored with the lightest of touches, including upgraded heating and services.

'The courtyard makes for a different kind of space, if you will, in the house,' says Jan Utzon, 'even though my father was not restricted to that because the land around the house was relatively extensive. He liked the courtyard as a nice outdoor space in a house. And it was spectacularly different from what had been done before architecturally, so we had lots and lots of architects coming by to have a look at the house. It influenced succeeding construction of warm, family houses in Denmark for quite a long while afterwards.'[3]

Opposite and right As well as the enclosed courtyard, the plan of the house, with its projecting bedroom wing, also offers a choice of patios and terraces, helping to dissolve the boundaries between outdoors and in.

501
FLORENCE
Arkitektur
HUSE
Matisse

Opposite and above The kitchenette and dining area in the original portion of the house have been purposefully preserved and retained, even though more spacious alternatives are now available in the additional part of the building.

Left The principal bedroom is in the private family wing in the new part of the house; the subject of the portrait is Jørn Utzon.

Didrichsen House & Museum

Art house elegance

Danish-born businessman Gunnar Didrichsen and his wife, Marie-Louise, shared a love of art and architecture. After Didrichsen settled in Helsinki during the late 1920s, he established a successful cosmetics company known as Transmeri and married the Swedish-speaking Finn Marie-Louise Granfelt, an office manager, in 1939. In the years after World War II the Didrichsens travelled widely in Europe and beyond, while beginning to collect pieces of art and sculpture that they both enjoyed and appreciated.

Over time, the Didrichsens' collection grew from its foundations in late nineteenth- and early twentieth-century Finnish painting to include works by such European modern artists as Pablo Picasso, Sonia Delaunay and Wassily Kandinsky, as well as sculpture by Jean Arp, Alberto Giacometti and particularly Henry Moore. The Didrichsens got to know Moore well, visiting the sculptor's home and studio in Perry Green, Hertfordshire. Art became a constant presence in the Didrichsens' own homes, especially their house on the island of Kuusisaari in western Helsinki, which the couple commissioned modernist Finnish architect Viljo Revell to design for them during the mid-1950s.

By this time, the Didrichsens owned a spacious apartment in the centre of the city and a summer cottage in Vuosaari further east along the coast. In turning to Revell to design their new family home, the couple were not only fully embracing a mid-century modern aesthetic but also taking the golden opportunity to create a home fully tailored to their needs, as well as those of their four young children and their growing art collection.

The Didrichsens originally approached Alvar Aalto to design the house, but he was already overcommitted to new projects and warmly recommended Revell, his former colleague, who had established his own practice and developed an innovative portfolio of work, including a number of villas and housing projects. The couple soon formed a close and collaborative way of working with Revell, discussing and developing ideas for the new house.

The first part of the project was a two-storey home, which was gently pushed into the sloping coastal site, overlooking the shore and placed among the pine trees. The principal, upper level holds the main entry sequence, leading through to a spacious and largely open-plan living area that incorporates a sitting room, library and dining area arranged around a central stairwell down to the lower-ground floor, as well as an indoor garden alongside it. There are many integrated elements, including library shelving and storage units, along with a custom-made music cabinet and, at the top of the staircase, a bespoke fitted bar contained in an elegant credenza. This upper storey also holds a separate kitchen, with maid's quarters beyond, and then a sequence of children's bedrooms facing the sea, connected by a spacious hallway that doubles as a play area. The primary bedroom, an additional living room and a sauna are situated on the lower-ground floor.

Then, during the early 1960s, as the couple's art collection began to evolve and expand, the idea of a new addition to the house cropped up at a party. 'It was on this occasion that artist Ragni Cawén came up with the idea of a separate gallery,' wrote Gunnar Didrichsen. '"You, Gunnar, who are so interested in art, should have a separate gallery for your art. As it is, the architecture suffers from the art, which also does not come into its own." I was indeed short of space, the hat rack in my wardrobe bulging with the weight of antique sculptures.... I went up to Revell, who was also present, and said "listen to Ragni Cawén". Instead of the dismissive response I had expected, he said, "That's a very interesting idea", and a few days later he came with some sketches.'[1]

The result was a new gallery on the landward side of the house, creating a fresh U-shaped plan for the building overall. Revell placed a swimming pool into the resulting courtyard space, while a reclining figure by Henry Moore sits between the pool and the pathway to the front door. The museum wing not only created valuable extra space for the couple's art collection but also lent the extended building a pleasing sense of cohesion, enhanced by the partially sheltered pool court and other additional outdoor spaces.

The provision of the new museum wing helped to create a U-shaped plan for the building, with a swimming pool situated alongside the gallery, and a sculpture by Henry Moore, *Reclining Figure on a Pedestal* (1960), positioned next to the pathway leading to the main entrance.

As well as continuing to develop their collection and establishing a foundation to manage it for the future, the Didrichsens also decided to open their new gallery to the public. Revell's new wing was completed in 1964 and first opened in 1965, with Marie-Louise Didrichsen devoting much of her time and energy to running the museum until she passed away in 1988. The museum, which continues to thrive, is still looked after by the family and a team of curators.

Revell, however, died of a heart attack the same year as the museum wing was completed, at the age of just 54. He was said to have been exhausted by the challenge of completing the most ambitious project of his career, Toronto City Hall, designed in conjunction with Canadian firm John B. Parkin Associates. 'He was an exceptionally sympathetic person and we liked him a lot,' said Gunnar Didrichsen, who lamented his loss, promising to keep the architectural integrity of his building unchanged. 'Revell was a very fine character.'[2]

Opposite and above left The bespoke fitted kitchen is complemented by a breakfast area alongside it, with a table by Revell and chairs by Ilmari Tapiovaara.

Above The dining room features a circular table by Revell and a 'miracle Sputnik' chandelier by Bakalowits & Söhne from 1962. The painting, *Silver-Grey*, by Ahti Lavonen, is owned by the Nordea Art Foundation.

DIDRICHSEN

PICASSO & CO.
ART NOUVEAU

Previous The original residence sits to the left of the courtyard and the gallery to the right, with the main entrance and a glass fronted link sitting between the two.

Opposite The main living area revolves around the stairwell to the lower level and an indoor garden alongside, with various zones placed around these elements, including the lounge and library.

Right and below The lounge includes sofas by Ahti Taskinen and armchairs by Kristian Vedel, while the painting by Leena Luostarinen, *Snake-Flower* (1986), belongs to the Nordea Art Foundation. Revell designed many integrated, bespoke features including the credenza bar and the pull-out gramophone in the library.

Gunnløgsson House

Mid-century waterside living

Jakob Halldor Gunnløgsson

Rungsted
Denmark

1958

The house opens up dramatically to views across the waters of the Øresund Strait, while the main living areas also flow out on to the terraces running the length of the building.

In 1957, Jakob Halldor Gunnløgsson celebrated his marriage and embarked on an extended honeymoon across Japan and Asia. The trip was to make a great impression on the Danish architect and his wife, Lillemor Gunnløgsson, the daughter of a Danish ship's captain. On their return, the subtle influence of Japanese architecture and design made a significant impact on Halldor Gunnløgsson's work, seen most explicitly in the new house that the architect designed for himself and Lillemor on the shores of the Øresund Strait.

The couple found a modest parcel of land by the sea at Rungsted, north of Copenhagen. The neighbourhood became fashionable during the nineteenth century and continued to evolve during the post-World War II period when the Gunnløgssons managed to secure the purchase of one of the last available sites belonging to the historic Hannelund Estate. The setting is certainly mesmerizing, offering direct access to the shoreline as well as open views eastwards across the Strait.

The only problem was the main coastal road from Copenhagen to Helsingør, which runs right beside the house to the west. To try and offset the presence of the road and create a sense of seclusion, Gunnløgsson planted a hedge along the boundary and then excavated the site to create a sunken plateau between the road and the shore. Here, the architect designed a discreetly placed, single-storey building with a timber frame, banks of glass and brick bookend walls at either end. The house has a flat roof coated in shingle, punctuated with skylights, and – given the careful design and placement of the building – is almost invisible from the road.

The influence of Japanese architecture and interior design is evident from the start. Gunnløgsson created a sheltered entrance porch within the linear outline of the building, backed by a row of black-painted timber doors that conceal a neat line of storage and service units. The porch leads to the front door and a modern interpretation of the genkan, or traditional Japanese hallway, where visitors can remove their coats and shoes, placing them in a lacquered cabinet with sliding doors that conceal the interior joinery, painted a vivid crimson red.

The hallway leads into a generous and largely open-plan living space with walls of glass on either side. The palette of materials is essentially natural in character, as well as textural, with the underheated floor coated in grey Kolmården marble tiles, which were leftovers from the architect's Tårnby Town Hall project (1959) that he was working on at around the same time. The expressed timber frame and wooden wall panelling are also painted black, while the ceilings are in pale, slatted wood strips.

A double-sided fireplace lightly separates the study to one side and the lounge to the other, situated on the seaward aspect of the building. The dining area sits within this fluid space as well, while the compact kitchen is placed within a central service core, which can be opened up or closed down using integrated sliding doors. Reminiscent of Japanese shoji screens, these flexible partitions can also section off the bedroom suite, alongside the dining area, as desired.

The only bedroom in the house, this suite features dark, lacquered wooden walls to the rear, with a bespoke bed in a matching finish. Gunnløgsson also designed a custom-made dressing table and storage box here, inspired by a sea captain's chest. The small bathroom, accessed via the bedroom, is top-lit by a skylight and also features marble floors.

Designed solely for the couple themselves, the house is modest in scale yet beautifully detailed and finished throughout. There are many other bespoke, fitted features, such as the bookcases and the fold-down table on the terrace facing the shore. Much of the loose furniture is by the Gunnløgssons' friend and neighbour, Poul Kjærholm, along with lighting by Le Klint. And while the house is modestly scaled and compact, the careful positioning of the building and the floor-to-ceiling glass walls overlooking the terrace and garden towards the Øresund Strait enhance the feeling of openness and the overall impression of space. In this respect, the panorama of the water and the sky becomes part of the house itself.

Japanese architecture and design also influenced a number of Gunnløgsson's Nordic contemporaries, including Finn Juhl and

Above The fireplace forms a focal point for the seating area while also acting as a partial point of separation within the open plan between the lounge and study space beyond.

Opposite The stone floors, timber ceilings and dark wooden walls help to unify the open-plan living area, while sliding partitions can be used to separate the bedroom suite and also the kitchen from the 'great room' as needed.

arguably Alvar Aalto. Although Aalto never visited Japan himself, he did refer to the country's architecture and interiors in his work, as seen in his own home and studio in Helsinki (1936), as well as in other projects.

Above and right There is a quality of simplicity, order and restraint to the house, which is almost Japanese in character, as seen in the entrance sequence, including the porch and entrance hallway, or genkan, with its integrated storage cupboards to one side.

Above The careful positioning of the low-slung, single-storey building on the site ensures discretion and privacy while also allowing the Gunnløgssons to maintain an open relationship with the coast and the Øresund Strait.

Bigaard Sørensen House

The new natural home

Brabrand
Denmark

1963

Integrated furniture and bespoke elements lend the interiors a sense of sophisticated simplicity, while the loose, mid-century pieces include the Spanish chairs around the coffee table by Børge Mogensen.

'Simplicity is our goal,' said Friis, 'not bragging shapes and façades. We allow houses to grow from the inside and let the shapes and façades be the result, rather than the prerequisite.'

Danish architects Knud Friis and Elmar Moltke Nielsen first met as students at Copenhagen School of Architecture. Following their graduation, the two friends stayed in touch even though Friis moved to Aarhus to take a position with C.F. Møller Architects, while Moltke stayed in Copenhagen to work with architect Jørgen Bo, who was one of his former tutors. By 1955, however, Moltke had also settled in Aarhus, on the eastern coast of Jutland, and the pair began working together on a number of small projects, including their first houses. A major commission for an apartment building provided the impetus for Friis and Moltke to launch their own architectural firm, based in Aarhus, by 1957.

Friis & Moltke's mid-century work was, for the most part, highly contextual, with their buildings forging strong links with their surroundings while working around the natural characteristics of the landscape. This was especially true of their hotels and houses, which included the architects' own innovative homes. Friis's family home in Brabrand, to the west of the city of Aarhus, offered one key exemplar, fusing a rigorous approach to structure and clearly expressed materiality with the realization of a strong relationship between inside and outside space, partly achieved through the use of a walled central courtyard with a studio to one side and private living spaces to the other.

Over the coming years, Friis & Moltke went on to design and build a rich portfolio of houses, with single-family residences becoming a vital strand of their work during the 1960s. 'Simplicity is our goal,' said Friis, 'not bragging shapes and façades. We allow houses to grow from the inside and let the shapes and façades be the result, rather than the prerequisite.'[1]

One of the most rounded and delightful of Friis & Moltke's mid-century homes is the Bigaard House, also situated in Brabrand. The clients were the interior designer Vivian Bigaard Sørensen and her husband, Bent Bigaard Sørensen, who commissioned a new home within a clearing among the trees, designed in 1961 and completed in 1963.

The single-storey house was placed gently in the wooded landscape. A key element of the design is a long, spinal brick wall that anchors the house to the site while also helping to define three complementary rectangular structures made of brick and timber. A simple garage and store stand to one side of the wall, closest to the driveway, while a second block across a cobbled courtyard comprises the main entrance, plus the modestly scaled principal suite.

The main body of the house sits behind the wall, where a much larger, linear pavilion holds the key living spaces, and banks of ceiling-to-floor glass windows look out onto the garden and the adjoining terraces.

Below Whitewashed brickwork accentuates the outline of the house against its woodland backdrop.

The living pavilion is largely open plan, although a central fireplace and its brick surround help to delineate the lounge and study at one end from the combined kitchen plus dining area at the other, even as the stone flag floors and timber ceilings help to create a sense of harmony and cohesion throughout.

Vivian Bigaard Sørensen collaborated with Friis & Moltke on the interiors, which include a number of bespoke design and integrated ingredients. The lounge, for example, revolves around a choice of two seating zones, with one by the fireside and another by the end wall of the house, where the brickwork is painted white, and a built-in sofa and coffee table both feature fixed brick bases. A study and library zone sits alongside the spine wall, with shelving and display units anchored to the brickwork.

Beyond the fireplace, at the other end of the pavilion, the kitchen and dining area has a bespoke character of its own. The wrap-around kitchen units and work surfaces have an ergonomic quality, making use of all available space, while the dining table is partly served by a fitted, wooden-slat bench fixed to the end wall of the house.

The sense of space is enhanced by the generosity of the windows feeding out to the terraces, which are either protected by the pavilion itself or the outstretched arms of the elongated spine wall. Clerestory windows and skylights enrich the quality of natural light within the principal spaces, where the use of organic materials of various kinds provides a complementary but cohesive range of textures and tones. The overall impression is one of tranquillity.

Although the principals of the practice passed on many years ago, Friis & Moltke continues to flourish today, along with a number of other long-established Danish firms. More recent projects have also forged a strong relationship between architecture and landscape, including Friis & Moltke's celebrated Hotel Føroyar on the outskirts of Tørshavn in the Faroe Islands.

Below The long, central spine wall helps to delineate the main living spaces from the bedroom pavilion and garage behind it

Below The brick base of the fitted sofa and the white brickwork of the end wall fuse together to create a pleasing sense of cohesion, while contrasting with the soft leather cushions.

Right The architects' model of the house shows the central spine wall with the main living pavilion facing the garden, while the bedroom pavilion and garaging are on the other side of the wall.

Below The fireplace and its dark hood contrast vividly and graphically with the brickwork of the chimney wall, which also serves as a partial partition between the sitting room and the kitchen.

Opposite The principal bedroom includes many fitted elements, such as the desk and shelving, adding to the restrained but pleasing treatment of the interiors.

Below and right The compact kitchen and dining area sit at one end of the main pavilion, where the doorway leads out to the adjoining terrace and garden.

Kamban House

A Faroese studio house

Sculptor Janus Kamban lived and worked in the city of Tórshavn for much of his life, becoming one of the most respected Faroese artists of his generation. He was born in the Faroese capital, where his father worked as a teacher, and grew up there at a time when Tórshavn – situated on the main island of Streymoy – was beginning to evolve from its roots as a trading town into a thriving Nordic city and cultural centre, helped by the expansion of its harbour and fishing fleet, and its ferry links to Denmark and Iceland.

Kamban's artistic talents were spotted early on by his mentor, the Danish-Faroese painter Gudmund Hentze, who suggested that Kamban should pursue an education in the arts. Like his Icelandic contemporary, Ásmundur Sveinsson (see pp. 82–87), Kamban went to Copenhagen to begin his studies, concentrating initially on painting before switching to sculpture and training at the Royal Academy of Fine Arts under Danish sculptor Einar Utzon-Frank during the 1930s. Around the same time, the young artist broadened his horizons by travelling to other parts of Scandinavia, as well as to France and Italy.

Following his graduation, Kamban went to work in Utzon-Frank's atelier, and began to exhibit his own work in Denmark. But his plan to return to the Faroe Islands was interrupted by World War II, when the islands were temporarily occupied by the British. The sculptor eventually managed to return to Tórshavn in 1945, with the Faroe Islands achieving home rule from Denmark and increased autonomy from 1948 onwards.

The 1950s and 1960s were an important period of cultural development in the Faroes, particularly in Tórshavn, and this was true of both the arts and architecture. One of Kamban's most famous works dates from 1948, when he created a memorial in the capital to Venceslaus Ulricus Hammershaimb, who first documented the Faroese language in written form during the nineteenth century. Kamban's work can also be seen at the Faroese National Library, designed by Tórshavn architect Jákup Pauli Gregoriussen, and at Listasavn Føroya, the National Gallery of the Faroe Islands, also designed by Gregoriussen, who was one of the most influential post-war architects working on the islands.

It was Gregoriussen, with whom Kamban had much in common, that the sculptor turned to when he decided to build his own home and studio in Tórshavn. Kamban settled on a hillside site on the green edges of the fast-growing city, with views across the nearby coastline towards the small island of Nólsoy in the distance. The resulting building fuses mid-century modern elements with vernacular Faroese references, particularly in the use of a traditional green turf roof on the saltbox roof, where the longer slope edges towards the adjoining street and the shorter pitch faces the sea.

The entire building is gently pushed into the hillside and accessed from the road to the rear. The bespoke, double-height studio sits at one end of the building, with a tall bank of windows looking seaward, complemented by skylights that help to maximize the quality of natural light. A double doorway to one side offers a useful, dedicated entrance to the studio space from the driveway alongside.

The rest of the house and its living spaces are arranged over three levels, with various changes in height and volume. The main entrance leads into a central hallway, which offers access to the studio to one side and the kitchen plus dining area to the other. From the pivotal hall, steps lead down to the bedrooms and bathroom, which have their own views facing eastwards. Yet, the most dramatic and welcoming space is undoubtedly the main sitting room on the upper level, accessed via a stairway leading up from the circulation hub.

This is a decidedly mid-century modern space, with an open-plan layout and ribbon windows framing the vista. The pitched roof and timber-clad ceilings offer a sense of height and openness, with space enough for a lounge and library at one end of the room, a feature fireplace against one wall towards the centre, and also a dining and work table at the opposite end. Despite the relatively urban context of Tórshavn, the feeling is still escapist within the living room in particular, given the open sea views, while the warm, organic

Janus Kamban's hillside home references the Faroese vernacular, featuring a green roof and other familiar traits, yet is also a decidedly mid-century modern building.

Jákup Pauli Gregoriussen & Janus Kamban

Tórshavn
Faroe Islands

1966

Kamban House

HAMMERSHØI

Opposite The double-height studio occupies one end of the building, with a large picture window facing the sea and complemented by skylights; the studio also has its own side entrance.

Left The house looks out eastwards towards the island of Nólsoy.

Below As seen from the central hallway, the house features various shifts in level, with the kitchen close to the main entrance, the bedrooms downstairs and the living room upstairs.

character of the house is enhanced by the extensive use of timber throughout.

Kamban lived and worked at the house from 1966 until his death in 2009, creating both sculptural pieces and prints, some of which can still be seen in the building. His work was modern in character yet also celebrated the landscapes, heritage and natural beauty of the islands, much as Gregoriussen sought to establish a fresh approach to Faroese architecture that was grounded in the islands' history. The artist's house is now cared for by the Faroese state and periodically made available to visiting artists.

Opposite The living room is on the uppermost level of the house, which enjoys the best views over the Tórshavn coastline and the sea beyond.

Above The living room is generously scaled with high, pitched ceilings and space enough for a dining/work table at one end and a seating area with a library of books at the other.

Futuro House

The home of the future

Perched among the trees within a quiet quarter of Espoo, on the outskirts of Helsinki, there is a bright glimpse of the future. A yellow dome, floating a few feet above the ground, the Futuro House was designed in the late 1960s by Finnish architect Matti Suuronen who wanted to change the world of house and home. This was house number one within a collection of prefabricated plastic cabins intended for mass production, with the futuristic saucers flexible enough to be delivered to site by lorry or helicopter. Futuro House 001 and its siblings were initially made by Finnish company Polykem at their factory around fifteen miles from Espoo, ready for delivery to clients such as actor, screenwriter and television personality Matti Kuusla, the original owner of house 001.

Delivered to Kuusla's country estate in Hirvensalmi, to the northeast of Helsinki, and placed on a hillside overlooking Lake Puulavesi, the first official Futuro was intended to grab media attention and generate publicity for Polykem's new prefab. Yet the bright-yellow bubble house also managed to alarm some of Kuusla's neighbours. 'I was amused by the outcry,' said Kuusla of House 001, now owned by the WeeGee Exhibition Centre in Espoo. 'I even heard that the local residents were plotting to blow it up with dynamite.'[1]

The story of Futuro dates back to the early 1960s, when Matti Suuronen was asked to design a low-cost ski cabin suited to remote mountain settings. The architect already had experience using fibreglass, having designed reinforced plastic domes for grain silos, and began working on a concept for a circular cabin, which was then developed further by Polykem, whose managing director, Ensio Söderström, saw a bright future in prefabricated cabins and other factory-produced micro buildings.

Working with a team of engineers and technicians, Suuronen developed his ideas for the Futuro, which became a rounded, elliptical saucer with an 8-metre (26-foot) diameter, made up of a total of sixteen segments of fibreglass plus sixteen neat oval windows in clear acrylic, along with another four at low level, making twenty in total. Suuronen added an airliner-style hatch that pulled down to reveal a set of access steps, leading into a small entrance hall with a compact toilet to one side. The main compartment of the Futuro held a central fireplace that doubled as a cooking grill, while to one side sat a sequence of six integrated chairs that could easily be adjusted and lowered to serve as beds, while there was also a galley kitchenette nearby. The design of the Futuro referenced boats and airplanes as much as cabin concepts but also built on the example of earlier prefabricated housing concepts such as Richard Buckminster Fuller's pioneering Dymaxion House, first designed in the late 1920s.

Having invented his flying saucer, one of Suuronen's remaining challenges was to work out how to hold it in place once it was delivered to site. The architect's solution was a steel ring beam that holds the Futuro like a cradle and is supported in turn by four steel legs anchored to the ground. 'First came the egg, then came the egg cup,' as Suuronen once put it.[2]

Polykem and Suuronen went on to develop an experimental prototype Futuro, known as House 000, followed by Kuusla's House 001. Then, in the autumn of 1968, Polykem exhibited Futuro House 002 at an export fair in London, where the saucer was mounted on an exhibition barge on the River Thames. Building on the attention gained from these initial houses, Polykem put Futuro into production and set up a series of licensing agreements with manufacturers abroad, including in the United Kingdom and the United States. New Futuros were sold for around $14,000 and also won a good deal of publicity, including a 1969 article in the *New York Times* published on the day of the Apollo 11 moon landing.

There were some significant successes for the Futuro. The famous Stockmann department store exhibited a full-sized saucer inside its central Helsinki headquarters in 1969, while the Swedish Air Force acquired a triptych of Futuros to serve as lookout posts that same year, famously using their helicopters to deliver them to site. During the late 1960s and early 1970s, Polykem even felt confident enough to expand its

The saucer-like fibreglass home, inspired by the design of boats and airplanes, sits on a steel ring beam with four supporting legs that hold the Futuro firmly in place.

Matti Suuronen

WeeGee Exhibition Centre
Espoo, Finland

1968

'Casa Finlandia' prefab range with additional designs, marketed for use as motel units, cafés, kiosks and pop-up shops.

It was the global oil crisis of 1973 and subsequent recession that ended the short-lived glory days of the Futuro. Suddenly, investment was in short supply while the cost of production using oil-based plastics rose sharply, sealing the end of production in Finland and overseas. Some estimates suggest that at least one hundred Futuros were made and, of these, around sixty plus survive in various countries.

The original prototype of the Futuro is now in the hands of the Boijmans Van Beuningen Museum in Rotterdam, while the WeeGee Exhibition Centre in Espoo acquired Kuusla's House 001 in 2011. The yellow saucer has been living among the trees next to the centre since 2012, serving as a reminder of a time of optimism and innovation, when anything seemed possible and the future was golden.

Below The Futuro was factory-made with fibreglass segments, with eight segments for the upper section and eight for the lower, which were then fixed together to create the circular structure.

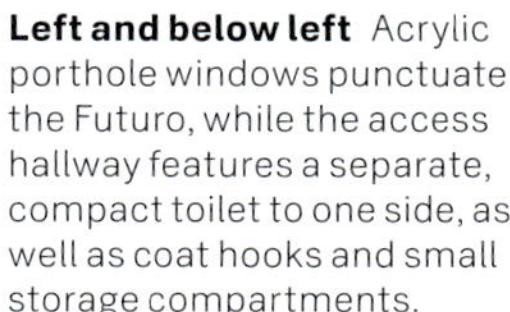

Left and below left Acrylic porthole windows punctuate the Futuro, while the access hallway features a separate, compact toilet to one side, as well as coat hooks and small storage compartments.

Below Access to the Futuro is provided by fold-down steps within an airline-inspired access hatch that sits flush to the hull when pushed upwards in its sealed position.

Above The main living space revolves around a central stove, surrounded by a series of fitted seats that can be adjusted to double as beds. A compact kitchenette sits alongside the entrance hall.

Above The internal hatch from the entrance hall through to the main compartment holds echoes of ship's doorways (left), while the folding steps take inspiration from the world of aviation (right).

Villa Schjøtt

A home within the landscape

Geir Grung

Bergen
Norway

1969

The angular geometry of the house, with its projecting roof plates and canopies, developed in response to the rugged topography of the site, contrasts with the rounded drum holding the staircase.

Norwegian modernist architect Geir Grung knew the neighbourhood of Tveiterås well. Situated in the south of Bergen, this green enclave was partly laid out by his father, architect Leif Grung, who also designed the family's own villa here, where his son grew up before studying in Oslo. During the 1960s, when Geir Grung's practice was at the height of its success, he was asked to return to Tveiterås to design a new home for his brother-in-law, businessman Helge Schjøtt.

While the neighbourhood is quiet, leafy and desirable, the rugged topography can be challenging, and such was the case with the hillside site that Schjøtt and his family settled on. The setting on the edge of a ridge, looking down into the valley below, helped to shape Grung's architectural design and the unusual form of the concrete and glass villa, which was pushed into the slope of the hill while making the most of the open views.

'The house is fitted to an extremely difficult site,' Grung explained in a self-published portfolio of key projects. 'The driveway is on the upper side and these requirements are the reason why the house has its very special shape. The house is built in Mexi-stone and concrete, with a dark-stained roof trim. Inside, there are carpets and tiles on the floor and a redwood ceiling.'[1]

The house was arranged over two floors, with the main entrance on the upper level and accessible from the drive adjoining the roadway situated behind the villa. This upper storey originally included the library, dining room and living room, arranged around a feature fireplace, as well as the primary bedroom, a compact kitchen and a substantial indoor swimming pool, with glass walls connecting it to an adjoining terrace.

A sculptural brick drum, topped by a skylight, offers access to the lower level with the children's bedrooms, a family bathroom and service spaces, including plant rooms and provision for the base of the pool. Overall, the outline of the house is angular in response to the shape of the hillside itself, although this is softened by the walls of glass facing the valley, as well as the external expression of the drum holding the staircase.

The use of the characterful drum to soften the geometry of the house might be compared with the way that Grung adopted similar elements in other residential projects, particularly his own home in Oslo, Villa Jongskollen, completed just a few years earlier in 1964. Circular forms also appear in a number of Grung's other commissions, such as the Ring office building in Oslo (1965).

In every respect, the villa offers a bespoke response both to the setting and the needs of Grung's clients. 'As an expert, an architect can easily lock his freedom of thought', Grung once said of his architectural philosophy. 'With this in mind I have always attempted individual solutions whatever the problem may be. Expression in architecture must be just as varied as each petal in a rose.'[2]

Villa Schjøtt is certainly a unique project within a rich and varied collection from the 1960s and 1970s, ranging from residences to hydroelectric power stations, office buildings, hotels and yachts. More recently, Grung's work has been rediscovered and celebrated, including the villa, which has been renovated and updated by designers Morten and Nina Michelsen, who also grew up in Tveiterås.

The Michelsens acquired the villa from the Schjøtt family, with the aim of revitalizing the building. One of the greatest challenges was presented by the swimming pool, which not only swallowed a substantial amount of space but, over the years, had leaked and compromised other parts of the house. The Michelsens eventually decided to remove the pool, which freed up additional living space across both floors of the house.

Upstairs, the removal of the pool and the gentle adjustment of the floor plan allowed for the creation of a much more spacious, open-plan living area as well as a larger custom kitchen, while connections to the adjoining terraces were also strengthened. Downstairs, additional living space was created, while services throughout were updated, including underfloor heating, fed by a ground-source heat pump, and integrated lighting systems, as well as new glazing. The overall sense of space has been dramatically enhanced during the renovations, along with reinforcing the sense of connection with the surroundings.

Left Brickwork and concrete combine and contrast at Villa Schjøtt, where views across the landscape are carefully framed.

Left and below The layers of concrete and brick, working in combination with the vivid lines of the balconies and terraces, lend the house a unique character with these different strata echoing the geology of the land in abstract form.

Below and opposite Recent renovations have extended the main living space into a part of the house once occupied by an indoor swimming pool, while maximizing the open views across the valley.

Right The top-lit circular staircase in whitewashed brick offers one of the most engaging elements of the house, contrasting with the angular lines of the principal living spaces.

ANNIE LEIBOVITZ

Kukkapuro Studio

Under one roof

‘As a youngster in the 1950s and ’60s, I did play with the thought of applying to study architecture at Otaniemi,’ said Kukkapuro, ‘but I hated algebra and solving equations was simply off-putting, so I thought never mind! I’ve always been an architect in a sense though, but from a furniture angle. All the glassfibre chairs that came after Karuselli were commissions by architects.’

The all-encompassing shell roof shelters Yrjö Kukkapuro’s studio and that of his wife Irmeli, as well as serving, for many years, as the family home; the main entrance is through the blue door.

During the late 1960s, a few years after finding success with his most famous chair design – the Karuselli (1964) – Finnish designer Yrjö Kukkapuro began work on a new home studio. Shared with his artist wife, Irmeli, and their young daughter, the new building had much in common with the Karuselli. It, too, was sculptural in form and functional in purpose, with an original, dynamic character that spoke of the future. It was a place for painting, for working and for inventing, serving as the focal point for family life from 1969 onwards.

For many years, the Kukkapuros worked from their townhouse in the neighbourhood of Töölö, close to the centre of Helsinki, where Yrjö developed many of his earliest designs. He invented the Karuselli (Finnish for ‘carousel’) chair in 1964, with its ergonomic fibreglass shell seat, upholstered in leather and sitting on a suspension bracket that was mounted in turn on a pedestal stem anchored to a robust steel base. The distinctive sling seat could also swivel, like a merry-go-round, leading to the memorable name of a design put into production by Gunnar Haimi and his furniture company from 1965 onwards. The Karuselli soon became an international success story, helped by an appearance on the cover of Gio Ponti’s *Domus* magazine in Italy in 1966.

Kukkapuro continued collaborating with Haimi over the years that followed and was given workshop space in the Helsinki factory. Yet, eventually, Yrjö and Irmeli decided to design and build a bespoke studio for themselves on a parcel of land sitting alongside a traditional home owned by Irmeli’s parents, situated in the neighbourhood of Kaunianen between Helsinki and Espoo to the west. Irmeli’s father not only gave them permission to build the studio but also offered them temporary use of the family home while he was away working on an assignment. With funding partly provided by Yjrö’s award of the prestigious Lunning Prize, the designer began sketching out ideas for the new building, reflecting his deep-rooted interest in modern architecture.

‘As a youngster in the 1950s and ’60s, I did play with the thought of applying to study architecture at Otaniemi,’ said Kukkapuro, 'but I hated algebra and solving equations was simply off-putting, so I thought never mind! I've always been an architect in a sense though, but from a furniture angle. All the glassfibre chairs that came after Karuselli were commissions by architects.'[1]

Kukkapuro collaborated on the design of the new building with structural engineer Eero Paloheimo, developing the idea of an overarching concrete shell canopy, anchored to the ground at three points. A sinuous wooden mould was carefully constructed, complete with supporting steelwork, and then the concrete was poured into the mould in situ to create a super-strong shell 8-cm (3-in) thick. This canopy sheltered a universal space, with banks of glass looking out onto the garden and the surrounding trees, while a vivid blue door offered a distinctive entrance to the studio. There were dedicated spaces for Yrjö's design work, but also an integrated atelier for Irmeli, as well as sleeping quarters for the family and a modest kitchen to one side. The challenge of providing a bathroom and toilet was solved with the addition of two large, translucent fibreglass tanks of a kind usually found on farmsteads. While Kukkapuro had incoporated insulation and underfloor heating, fed by a basement boiler, he forgot to include ceiling lights, leading to the invention of his Valaisin 100 series of easily adaptable, freestanding spotlights, which was launched in 1968.

As intended, this universal space was also highly flexible. It served as both atelier and home, yet also provided a photographic studio for documenting new designs and a base for launching new products to buyers and the press. The studio was also well suited to entertaining, with the terrace to one side serving as an outdoor room. The Kukkapuros' studio became famous in its own right, with their daughter Isa recounting how a letter from Japan reached them simply addressed to: 'Yrjö, Kaunianen, Finland'.[2]

Eventually, the Kukkapuros decided to add another building alongside to serve as their main residence, while the studio was preserved as a place of work and invention. It continues to host Yrjö Kukkapuro's extensive archive of chairs and other designs, invented over the course of a long and highly productive lifetime.

Above Within the open-plan space under the shell roof, the Kukkapuros created a collection of different zones for working and living, with a rich quality of natural light provided throughout by the banks of glass that fill the gaps between the canopy and the ground.

Below The extensive glazing offers a vivid sense of connection between the building and the surrounding gardens, where the Kukkapuros eventually built an additional dwelling.

Right The entrance hallway, alongside the blue door, is partly defined by banks of storage to one side and two agricultural silos to the other, which were adapted to provide a toilet cubicle and a compact shower room.

Opposite Among the many pieces by Yrjö Kukkapuro within the studio house, one of the key designs is the famous Karuselli Chair and Ottoman, which made the designer famous.

Above The thin concrete shell structure has a leaf-like quality, enhanced by its position among the trees and within the garden site. The crescent-shaped terrace provides a partially sheltered outdoor room alongside the studio house.

Above The studio is home to a collection of Yrjö Kukkapuro's work, particularly his chairs.

Opposite Artist Irmeli Kukkapuro had a dedicated space of her own within the studio, where she concentrated primarily on lithographs, woodcuts and graphic art.

Galleria Rotunda
IRMELI KUKKAPURO
VALOSTA JA TILASTA
LJUS OCH RYMD
13.6.–2.10.1986

Nurmesniemi House & Studio

A harmonious live-work fusion

Antti & Vuokko Nurmesniemi

Kulosaari
Finland

1975

The mezzanine living room offers the best views over the coastal setting to the east of Helsinki. The reclining chairs were designed by Antti Nurmesniemi.

'The crisp geometrical outline contrasts with the richness of the interiors in terms of multiple shifts in level as well as changes in height, volume and scale.'

'A true home is created by living in it,' said Finnish furniture and industrial designer Antti Nurmesniemi.[1] The waterfront home that he shared with his wife, textile designer Vuokko, pays testament to his words, with its many layers of texture, colour, pattern, art and books, as well as their own contributions to the architecture and interior design of their home and studio. The result is a characterful and engaging setting for both daily living and work, with views across the bay framed by a line of pine trees that helps to shelter the home.

The building sits on the island of Kulosaari, which forms a leafy eastern neighbourhood of Helsinki. Although it is only a twenty-minute drive from the centre of the city, the couple's home sits within tranquil surroundings, bordered by mature trees, while the spaces between allow views over the inlet alongside. The Nurmesniemis acquired the site during the early 1970s and Antti – who was an interior architect, as well as a furniture and industrial designer – planned the house himself. Assisted by structural engineer Eero Paloheimo, he used a steel frame to create a geometric, rectangular building with expanses of glass connecting the inside to the garden, terraces and landscape. The private home is at one end and the design studio at the other, which was primarily used by Antti as his atelier and included a separate entrance of its own.

The crisp geometrical outline contrasts with the richness of the interiors in terms of multiple shifts in level as well as changes in height, volume and scale. The fully expressed steel-framed ceiling enhances the overall character of the building and serves as a unifying element, along with the use of white ceramic floor tiles on the lower levels and wooden floors upstairs, as well as timber joinery for the stairs to the mezzanine and other integrated elements. The interiors represent one of the fullest and most accomplished collaborations between Antti and his wife, the celebrated textile and fashion designer Vuokko, who famously worked with Marimekko during the 1950s before founding her own company, Vuokko Oy, in 1964. 'My husband Antti supported me in everything,' says Vuokko. 'He was so creative and multifaceted – the pillar of my life. We were partners for life, as well as close colleagues.'[2]

At the west end of the house, there is a double-height entrance hall and dining space, separated by a partially sunken and semi-enclosed kitchen. Towards the centre, there is a shift to two distinct storeys, with a library, swimming pool and sauna at lower-ground level and then a mezzanine living area, plus the adjoining principal bedroom, on the floor above. Arranged around a pivotal fireplace, the living room overlooks the dining area to one side, as well as offering a view of the studio – via an internal window – to the

other. The studio itself is, again, double height but also features a sunken storage and work zone to one side, with a secret door offering a hidden connection to the private realm of the house.

The house has many bespoke elements and integrated pieces of furniture, including the kitchen, the sauna, storage cupboards and the many banks of bookcases, which help to partition various zones within the house. There are also many pieces of furniture by Nurmesniemi, such as his famous, horseshoe-shaped Sauna Stool of 1952, initially designed for the Palace Hotel when he was working in the office of celebrated Finnish modernist architect Viljo Revell (see p. 96). Not long after, in 1956, Nurmesniemi established his own atelier and began a long and successful career that embraced furniture and product design, for example, his much-loved and highly colourful Pehtoori Coffee Pots and cookware for Wärtsilä dating from 1957 onwards.

Other key pieces in the house include the prototype for Nurmesniemi's 'Finlandia' modular sofa, for Vilka Oy, which sits in the living room by the fireplace, as well as the 'Triennaali' dining chairs produced by Piiroinen Oy, which were first presented at the Milan Triennale of 1960, winning a gold medal. Many of these designs still feel fresh and contemporary: 'A designed object does not need to reflect the times', said Antti Nurmesniemi. 'It is much better if it offers a hint of the future.'[3]

Later, the Nurmesniemis – who first met as students at the Ateneum art school in Helsinki – balanced their own careers with multiple collaborations on various projects, such as the 'Bubble on the Beach' stool of 1967, which featured a textile-patterned cushion by Vuokko. Other joint designs include the collection of striped armchairs and loungers developed for Vuokko Oy from the late 1960s onwards.

Above The house sits by the water's edge on the island of Kulosaari, where a line of fir trees offers a degree of privacy and shade, while softening the linear geometry of the house.

Opposite A terrace sits in front of the steel-framed home; the outdoor furniture is by Antti Nurmesniemi for Vuokko Oy.

Left and opposite The main living areas of the house are punctuated by pieces designed by Antti and Vuokko Nurmesniemi, including collaborations such as the 'Bubble on the Beach' stool and the striped Model 004 Armchair.

Many of the couple's designs, including their range of garden furniture, are still produced by Vuokko Oy, which is now run by Vuokko's niece, Mere Eskolin. Textiles and cushions by Vuokko feature throughout the house, along with her ceramics and glassware, for which the designer is also much respected.

The house is layered with many other personal treasures collected by the couple on their travels and over the decades. These include the Nurmesniemis' extensive book collection, lighting and choice pieces of work by a range of other modernist designers, such as Marcel Breuer's Wassily Chair, which sits in one corner of the elevated living room. Yet, at the same time, the inspirational beauty of the surroundings remains always at hand, with the interiors offering constant views of the natural world of the waterlands and the bay just beyond the boundaries of the garden.

Right and below The house accommodates multiple shifts in level, balancing open-plan living with the invention of distinct zones suited to different uses (right). Antti's iconic Sauna Stool can be seen among a collection of ceramics by Vuokko (below).

Below The mezzanine living at the centre of the plan floats above a library, where a workstation sits alongside banks of fitted storage units, as well as a doorway leading through to the work studio.

Villa Holme

A Norwegian new natural home

'The architect's role', Sverre Fehn once said, 'is to find the secret of the place.'[1] Much of the Norwegian master architect's work was focused on this search for the genius loci and the challenge of finding an accommodation between architecture and nature itself. This was true of the many houses that Fehn designed over the course of a long career, including Villa Holme, one of his last residential projects to be completed. Situated on the outskirts of the small coastal village of Holmsbu, around an hour's drive south of Oslo, the house certainly offers a unique response to a very specific and enticing setting.

The house was actually designed during the early 1970s for artist and graphic designer Ingolf Holme, yet construction was repeatedly delayed and postponed, with Holme only completing the building, with Fehn's blessing, in 1996. Holme not only wanted a residence but also a studio, which – along with the landscape itself – helped to influence the unusual composition of the building.

The site is at the foot of a steep granite cliff, softened by shrubs and pine trees, facing a gentle, wooded valley with hills beyond. Simply put, Villa Holme is a two-storey box but one that Fehn has subverted and adapted in various ways, as he positioned the square form diagonally within this landscape. The architect placed a single-storey outrigger to one side, holding the main entrance and a hallway (reminiscent of a Japanese genkan), while the prow of the main building was also scaled up and extended outwards to create a more spacious kitchen area on the ground floor, with the bathroom directly above it.

This subversion of pure geometry creates a building of engaging surprises from the start, while Fehn contrasted raw concrete surfaces for the exteriors with vertical timber cladding. Virginia creepers have softened these elevations over time, adding an array of natural colour tones, while the space between the house and the cliff to the rear is occupied by a spacious terrace, which serves as an outdoor room partly sheltered from the coastal breeze.

Internally, the plan presents a series of powerful axial lines and dynamic spaces. To the rear of the angled cube, Fehn created a triangular, double-height studio space that occupies almost one half of the footprint of the building, while offering – as the architect put it – 'neutral' light drawn from banks of windows facing the terrace and the rugged cliff face. The remainder of the fluid ground floor is also open plan, yet the other living spaces around the studio are still very clearly defined, with the lounge focused around a corner fireplace, surrounded by furniture of Fehn's own design. The dining area sits under the timber ceilings supporting the half level above, while the kitchen in the prow is arranged around a bespoke concrete island anchored to a supporting pillar, with additional surfaces and storage placed between a corner window looking out over the valley.

A sculptural spiral staircase leads to the mezzanine gallery and Holme's study, all overlooking the studio, and now home to a sequence of the artist's geometric works. Beyond the gallery, there are two similar bedrooms, each having its own doorway to the shared bathroom, where the bath is also placed on the diagonal, facing the window, with matching sinks to either side.

'The client has demonstrated enormous enthusiasm for the house and has followed the construction process with the artist's professional sense of precision,' said the Pritzker Prize-winning architect. 'One question will remain when you study Holme's paintings: is it the geometry of the house that has influenced his production, or have his pictures subconsciously controlled the architect's design?'[2]

Villa Holme is now under the guardianship of new owners, who have carefully maintained the building while preserving many of the original ingredients, including both custom elements and freestanding furniture by Fehn, as well as artworks by Ingolf Holme. The house still offers a prime example of the way in which Fehn sought to read the language of the landscape and respond accordingly.

With its backdrop of mature trees and a gentle coating of creepers, Villa Holme has gradually settled into the unique landscape that helped to inspire its creation.

Sverre Fehn

Holmsbu
Norway

1998

Opposite The space between the rocky hillside and the rear of the combined home and studio is inhabited by a semi-sheltered courtyard, where the terrace offers as an outdoor dining area in the warmer months.

Above and left With its outdoor spaces, indoor-outdoor connectivity and gentle planting around the building, the house engages with its surroundings and the views, while the combination of concrete and timber cladding helps it blend into the environment.

Opposite The corner fireplace is a key focal point within the house with Fehn's seating arranged around it, the mezzanine gallery running above it and the double-height studio to the left.

Above The kitchen sits within the prow of the building, looking out over the surrounding landscape, complemented by a bespoke concrete island around a supporting pillar, which forms a dramatic sculptural feature in itself.

Above right The double-height studio offers zones for both relaxing and working, while the tall bank of glass to the rear provides a rich quality of natural light and frames a vista of the rugged, rising hillside.

Left The building was intended as a painting studio as well as a home, with Fehn's design offering an ingenious and graphic solution to the challenge in the way that the double- and single-height sections of the structure define these two different functions.

Left The mezzanine gallery offers a place for displaying Holme's graphic artworks while also serving as an open landing leading to the elevated study overlooking the studio as well as two separate bedrooms.

Below The dining area is close to the kitchen and living room, forming one of three zones within the open-plan living space that sits beneath the ceilings of the partial upper level.

Hof House

Between the mountains and the sea

The house nestles gently into the pasture, while the owner's horse ranch can be seen further up the valley with a view of the glacial landscape in the far distance.

'The attraction of the site was that it was empty, exposed and free of any man-made constraints.'

The Hof House nestles in a mesmerizing landscape, sitting among the green pastures that form a hinterland between the mountains and the sea. Set sensitively and discreetly within these picturesque surroundings, the house has the feel of a comfortable and protective modern nest, echoing the instincts of the Arctic terns and other birds that also make their homes in these grasslands. This unique location first captured the affections of artist and horse breeder Lilja Pálmadóttir as a child when she visited her grandparents at the farmstead.

'I have always felt a deep connection to this place,' says Pálmadóttir, who shares the house and ranch with her family. 'My father grew up here but sold the farm, with deep regret, because he was so busy with his work. But I was lucky enough to buy it back in 2002 and started building the whole thing up again. And instantly, I decided that I wanted to build my own house here.'

The history of the settlement and the nearby village of Hofsós, situated on the shores of the Skagafjörður fjord, dates back many centuries. The oldest building on the farmstead today is the church, which was built in the late nineteenth century and has been recently restored, while Pálmadóttir has added new stables and a riding hall. There is also the traditional red house where her grandparents lived, which Pálmadóttir wanted to leave untouched by the construction of her new home, with the site carefully chosen to make the most of key vistas.

'I studied fine art, but I was always very interested in architecture and so I looked at the site thoroughly, trying to decide on the best place to build the house,' she explains. 'One day I was pacing back and forth, looking at all the different angles and the views, and I stopped where the kitchen sink is now. I looked deep into the valley to the east and then I turned around and saw the island in the fjord to the west. So I called Steve Christer at Studio Granda and said that I had found the perfect spot.'

Pálmadóttir had known Christer and his practice for some time, having created a mural for her older brother's house, which Studio Granda updated and extended during the 1990s. Their working relationship continued with their collaboration on the Hof House, which took two years to design and then another two years to build, beginning from the starting point of what was to become the kitchen sink.

'The attraction of the site was that it was empty, exposed and free of any man-made constraints,' says Christer. 'It was obvious that almost anything that was built there would, in all probability, make it less of a place than it already was but we could see that the chosen site has clear sight lines to the village and the island of Drangey, the headland and also the long valley, Unadalur. These were used as the focal points to orient various spaces in the house in a parallel manner to how the path of the sun was used as a planning tool.'

The design evolved over the course of many conversations. From the kitchen and dining area, sitting on the axial line with the two key vistas to either side, Studio Granda established a floor plan that incorporated an integrated, open lounge within this central living space, as well as a separate sitting room alongside it. Other key parts of the house, such as the main entrance sequence, radiate from this heartland, including the bedroom wing, which is accessed down a curvaceous, tunnel-like corridor. The house is arranged on one level while referencing the vernacular in a number of ways, for example, the turf that was carried from the pasture onto the green roof of the house.

'There wasn't at any stage a conscious attempt to make a modern turf house, but rather the design emerged from the nature of the site and the needs of Lilja and her entourage,' says Steve Christer. 'The discussion was more about carving, compression, light, darkness and tactility.'

The house was gently embedded in the landscape and used key materials such as concrete, exposed oak beams and wooden ceilings, along with a combination of cedar and recycled telegraph poles, found on site, for parts of the cladding where the raw concrete is not fully exposed. A key discovery early in the construction process was a foundation of basalt hiding under the pasture, with these dark hexagons of stone excavated and then laid throughout the interiors, offering a striking way of tying the main living spaces

Below Folded into the existing landscape and topped with a grass roof, the new building makes use of a range of materials, including concrete, cedar cladding and recycled telegraph poles for the end wall, The pathway to the main entrance can be seen to the right.

together, while oak floors were chosen for the bedrooms.

Given the extreme winters here, when the farmstead can be snowed in, high standards of insulation and glazing were woven into the fabric of the house throughout. Served by local geothermal energy and warmed by underfloor heating, the house has green credentials, although Christer and Pálmadóttir point out that such a strong focus on sustainability is not at all unusual in Iceland. The interior design and furniture choices were led by Pálmadóttir with a mixture of mid-century pieces and more contemporary ingredients.

'I really wanted to focus on Icelandic designs for this house, because for me it's an Icelandic house, not a Danish house,' says Pálmadóttir. 'The whole concept is about digging into our roots. The design evolved organically around the views – the valley, the mountains, the island – but this place is harsh in the winters and the winters you will not believe. So we really wanted to balance being able to feel the space of nature around you with the feeling of being sheltered and protected. It is a delicate balance.'

Below The new house is the latest addition to the family-owned farmstead, where Lilja Pálmadóttir has also added new stables and a riding hall, as well as renovating existing buildings.

Left While the house is partially embedded in the landscape, it still offers an engaging sense of connection with the natural surroundings via the large picture windows.

Opposite The use of hexagonal slabs of basalt, sourced on site, helps to unify the interiors, including the kitchen and the adjoining dining room, as well as reappearing in the bathrooms.

Opposite The lounge, with its focal fireplace, sits to one side of the open-plan living space at the centre of the house; the sofa is by Sveinn Kjarval and the two armchairs by Gunnar Gudmundsson.

Right The hexagonal basalt floors carry through into the passageway that links the main living spaces and the bedroom wing to one side of the house.

Below The main sitting room is a separate space, offering views across the landscape towards the coast, as well as the nearby barns, which have been partly coated in mirrored glass.

Árborg Villa

An Icelandic hilltop haven

The essential points of inspiration for the Icelandic architect Pálmar Kristmundsson are landscape and geology. Such references are threaded through his portfolio, which ranges from family homes to high-rise housing, as well as larger commissions such as the Embassy of Iceland in Berlin. Natural stonework features prominently in PK Arkitektar's work, along with layers of concrete that are treated in a similar manner, offering echoes of the rugged, natural terrain and tectonics of Iceland itself. Such themes are explored in depth in the design of the Árborg Villa, situated on a mossy hillside overlooking the River Hvitá to the south of the island.

Around a two-hour drive east from Reykjavík, the villa forges an intimate and multilayered relationship with the surrounding landscape. Stone and gravel from the valley were added to the mixture of bush-hammered concrete used to construct the house, with the aggregates showing through in the textural surface of the building. At the same time, river stones were used in the water pool bordering the terrace, while the green roof is coated in moss recovered from the site during the construction process and then carefully reinstated on top of the building. In these various ways and others, the villa connects itself to its setting and surroundings.

'In this case, the location accounts for the most powerful element,' says Kristmundsson. 'All I did was respond to the natural environment of the site. When we designed the Árborg Villa, I said that there shouldn't be any paint and no plasterboards. I preferred natural materials and an honest treatment of surfaces – a material palette that was connected to the site and the atmosphere.'[1]

The villa was commissioned by clients that Kristmundsson already knew well, having previously designed a house in Reykjavík for them. The new villa was intended as a vacation home to serve the needs of three generations: parents, grown-up children and grandchildren. With this in mind, generously scaled living spaces were required, along with a flexible layout that would accommodate the family.

'My first reaction was to think about two or three platforms, but the clients' request was to be all on one level,' says Kristmundsson. 'So the final response was one deck with an impression of the landscape, overlooking the bend in the river, with the house imitating the cliff and the rocks on the site.'[2]

Accessed from the brow of the hill, the villa has a carefully ordered entry sequence from the rear of the building. The main entrance is partially defined by the garage and storage block on one side, with a courtyard terrace behind it, and then the bedroom wing on the other, with a long and inviting hallway running between them. This processional sequence leads towards the internal threshold of the home and a wall of glass framing the open vista across the winding river, with the mountains in the far distance.

Having reached this key junction, turning right leads to the primary suite as well as another corridor offering access to three additional family and guest bedrooms within the private wing. Turning left, the villa opens up dramatically, with an open-plan living space holding the kitchen, dining area and lounge, anchored by a corner fireplace. This part of the house has the feel of a glass-sided pavilion, with generous banks of floor-to-ceiling glass to the front facing the open views of the valley. Walls of glazing also connect with the rear courtyard as well as another spacious and partly sheltered terrace at the far end of the house, complete with a plunge pool.

The use of renewable energy, in the form of geothermal, enhances the green credentials of the project, while other key materials include teak for the deck, which will weather grey over time. The flora and fauna around the house, including the moss and heather, have also been protected and preserved as far as possible, with Kristmundsson likening the construction process to gently lifting the landscape, slotting the villa into it, and then carrying the blanket of moss back over the building.

The choice of materials for the interiors contrasts the exposed, fair-faced concrete walls with an extensive use of teak and timber,

The house sits on the brow of the hill, which offers a dramatic vantage point overlooking the landscape, including the river estuary meandering through the valley below.

PK Arkitektar

Árborg
Iceland

2009

with wooden floors and ceilings, as well as crafted joinery for many integrated elements, such as storage cupboards and the bespoke kitchen. There is a sense of purity, tranquillity and restraint exhibited throughout, which is somewhat reminiscent of Japanese architecture. Certainly, Japan is a place where the architect spent some time following his studies in Denmark, with the country's architecture and design remaining a constant source of reference ever since. Yet, for Kristmundsson, the key lesson he brought back home from Japan was the importance of the relationship between architecture and nature, as seen so vividly at the Árborg Villa.

'It's always intriguing to get new perspectives on things', Kristmundsson says. 'In the town where I come from, there was not a single house that was oriented towards the landscape or a certain view. They're types that have been dropped down on a plot. So what was interesting for me was to see how the Japanese house responded to the landscape. I have reached an understanding that the environment should lead you in the design process. That's the goal and it's about making the most of the environment in which you find yourself.'[3]

Above The house possesses a strong tectonic personality, with its various layers and strata suggesting a geological quality that echoes the rugged character of the southern Icelandic landscape.

Left and above Vertical striations on the concrete surfaces of the building enhance the textural quality of the architecture, while creating vibrant contrasts with the layered strata of the house.

Above The main living area is a generously scaled, open-plan space with the kitchen and its island at one end, a dining area towards the centre and a lounge at the opposite end. The floor-to-ceiling glass frames the dramatic vista of the valley.

Opposite The interiors contrast the use of raw concrete surfaces with the extensive use of teak and other timbers, as seen in the floors, ceilings and joinery, including the integrated storage that lends the house a minimalist aesthetic.

Below The lounge forms part of the open-plan great room, while also leading out to the semi-sheltered terrace alongside; the sofas in the lounge are by Gianfranco Frattini for Tacchini.

Below The primary suite is in one corner of the house, overlooking the valley, while a sequence of family bedrooms sits beyond it within a sleeping wing that stretches back over the hillside.

Fjällbacka House

A cubist coastal composition

Gert Wingårdh

Fjällbacka
Sweden

2009

It is the maritime setting, above all, that draws Andrew Duncanson and Isaac Pineus to Fjällbacka. Situated on Sweden's western coast, around a ninety-minute drive north of Gothenburg, Fjällbacka's coastline is punctuated with islands and inlets where Duncanson, Pineus and their two sons enjoy sailing in the warmer months. In the summer, the family's Fjällbacka retreat, designed by the Gothenburg-based architect Gert Wingårdh, certainly comes into its own.

'The village is very picturesque but for us it's the archipelago outside of Fjällbacka that is really interesting,' says Duncanson, who runs the Modernity furniture gallery together with his husband. 'The children are good sailors so we will take our boat out to one of the islands, close to the coast, and we can have the whole island to ourselves for the day, which is a luxury. So if we are here in Fjällbacka and the weather is good, then it's an island day. We will pack a picnic, go out early in the morning and perhaps even have dinner on one of the islands on the way home.'[1]

Scottish-born Duncanson and Pineus first met in Stockholm, where they have an apartment, as well as one of the two Modernity galleries (with the second in London). They have been coming to Fjällbacka for many years, given that Pineus has family links here and both his parents and sister have summer homes next door. Initially, they shared a cabin with Pineus's sister but eventually thought that they needed a dedicated space of their own.

'We started to look for somewhere but then we started looking at this site just alongside the two other houses,' Duncanson says. 'Isaac's grandparents had bought it so that no one else would build there and it was just this wooded garden. But then we all started to look into it further and thought maybe it could work and perhaps we could build a house there after all.'[2]

The garden site sits within a gentle bowl in the landscape, bordered by grass banks and boulders. This natural dip in the topography means that the sea views are limited but, on the other hand, the setting provides instant protection from the sea breezes that sometimes run down the coastline. Embracing the opportunity to build a home on such a sheltered spot meant that Pineus and Duncanson could fully explore the ideal of a vivid indoor-outdoor relationship, while creating terraces and outdoor rooms around the summer residence.

They approached Wingårdh, who is well known for his innovative summer houses and rural escapes, as well as larger cultural and commercial projects. The architect knows the west coast well, and he and his wife have a summer house of their own further south. Wingårdh began working on designs that would balance the need for shelter with a vivid sense of connectivity with the surroundings. At the same time, the architect wanted to offer spaces where the sea view could still be appreciated, leading to a two-storey building with a roof terrace facing the coast.

'Early on, I subdivided the house into three parts, including the two-storey part on one side of the staircase and then the single-storey section on the other, with high ceilings and a hidden roof terrace on top of it,' says Wingårdh. 'But I wanted to add another layer and so we introduced the brise-soleil boxes that shield the extensive glazing, with two serving as terraces for seating. In the end, it's just a nice composition and the exposed wood on the outside has now weathered and taken on a concrete-like grey colour.'[3]

These strong cubic elements help to frame the three key elements of the house, while lending the front elevation a strong and distinctive character of its own, as well as helping to reinforce the indoor-outdoor relationship. Although the house was actually designed before the couple's two sons were born, the two-level part of the building offers a neat provision of children's bedrooms on the ground floor with the primary suite positioned above, while the stairway tower also leads upwards to the roof terrace.

The other part of the house holds a spacious great room, with banks of floor-to-ceiling glass connecting with the boxed terrace and looking out to the garden. With its broad planked wooden floors and high ceilings, this generously scaled space holds the kitchen

The projecting cubic boxes at the front of the house help to define key spaces within the building yet also provide protective porches that are partly sheltered from the elements.

and dining area at one end and the lounge, arranged around the fireplace, at the other. It also provides a welcoming setting for Duncanson and Pineus's collections of art and furniture, including Nordic designs – for which Modernity is best known – as well as a number of Italian pieces by Vico Magistretti and Gio Ponti, while a Mama Cloud chandelier by Frank Gehry floats over the Mario Bellini dining table.

'My family is from Scotland so if anybody was visiting we wanted to have some space for them and to have a dining room big enough to cope with a reasonable amount of guests,' says Duncanson. 'And we have always appreciated kicking down the boundaries between the outside and inside, which is why the windows are so big and we like to open up the doors. With these fishing villages along the coast, the houses are often piled up on top of one another, so for us the advantage is the amount of land around us and having a summer house that is pretty unique.'[4]

Right The main living area is a welcoming, open-plan space well suited to both family living and entertaining, while connecting with the adjoining porch via a wall of glass; the sofa is by Vico Magistretti.

Below The roof terrace offers views out over the nearby rocks and vegetation to the coastline spread out beyond.

Above and opposite Frank Gehry's Mama Cloud chandelier offers a focal point at the heart of the great room, floating over a dining table by Mario Bellini while the Superleggera dining chairs are by Gio Ponti.

Above right The red wall denotes the central atrium holding the staircase, which carries upwards to the principal suite and then up again to the roof terrace.

Above and opposite The furniture in the principal bedroom includes a plywood chair and nesting tables by Danish mid-century furniture designer Grete Jalk.

Above right The primary suite consists of the bedroom, bathroom and also a sauna with a view out across the garden towards the coast.

Bøe & Møller House

Japanese influences with art world inspiration

Knut Hjeltnes

Oslo
Norway

2014

The soothing sitting room has been designed around the fitted fireplace, feature windows and a large painting by Harald Fenn, while the mix of furniture includes pieces by Poul Kjærholm, Hans Wegner and Isamu Noguchi.

There is a longstanding synergy between Scandinavian and Japanese architectural design, particularly when it comes to house and home. This can be seen in the work of mid-century masters such as Finn Juhl (see p. 72) and Jakob Halldor Gunnløgsson (see p. 104), but also in residences designed by contemporary architects such as Knut Hjeltnes, for whom Japanese design is an important source of inspiration. It is one of the many threads and points of reference seen at Hjeltnes' Bøe & Møller House to the west of Oslo, designed for a Norwegian-Danish couple, Ketil Bøe and Marianne Moller.

'There is an atmosphere in those traditional Japanese houses, which I really appreciate,' says Hjeltnes, who has visited the country many times. 'It is a constant point of reference, among others, because I think a house should be a refuge and creating a sense of tranquillity is my main aim.'[1]

It was an interest shared by the architect and his clients, expressed at the house not only in the overall sense of calm but also in the use of crafted materials, organic textures and the integration of a Japanese-style entrance hall, or genkan, as well as sliding screens that help ensure an important sense of flexibility throughout. At the same time, there is an important relationship between house and garden, which is relatively enclosed and bordered by mature trees, creating a verdant enclave that adds to the secluded, escapist character of the home.

Bøe and Møller have lived in the same neighbourhood for many years, bringing up their two children there, but had begun to outgrow their previous home nearby. They noticed the site of their new home coming up for sale, complete with a flawed house dating back to the 1940s. The couple, who share a strong interest in art, architecture and design, seized the opportunity to acquire the site with the aim of creating a bespoke, modern home.

'We wanted something different to the typical houses that you see around here and to have that close connection to the garden, which we didn't have in the other house,' says Bøe, a solicitor. 'We also liked the idea of having everything on the same level, connecting with the outside, although still having some differences between the spaces to make it more interesting. The other thing, for us, was the uniformity of the materials to make sure that the house felt calm but also organic, warm and intimate. It was a good meeting of minds because Knut's points of inspiration worked well for us.'[2]

The existing basement of the former house was retained, providing storage and service spaces, including equipment for the ground-source heat pump that serves the underfloor heating and provides hot water. While the house is largely arranged on one level within a pin-wheel plan, there are multiple shifts in floor level that enable spaces to feel distinct and characterful in their own right, while still offering connectivity between them. The route through the house begins with the genkan, alongside the garage, where a fitted bench allows for shoes to be removed and stored, while a walk-in closet alongside offers storage for coats and outerwear. A sliding screen opens up to reveal the main dining area – a generous space with an angled aspen ceiling and connections to the kitchen to one side as well as a partially sheltered terrace to the other.

Beyond this, a few steps lead downwards to the sitting room, which is at right angles to the dining room, yet still has a direct relationship and link between the two spaces. This welcoming, quiet retreat was partly designed around the fireplace but also around a series of paintings by Harald Fenn. Collected over time by the couple, the works include a substantial, large-scale piece that forms a key element within the room, complemented by three other pieces by the same artist. Here, and elsewhere, the brick floors and walls – which are finished in a thin layer of plaster-like cement – are enhanced by many integrated, custom ingredients, such as the fitted bench by the fireplace and discreet storage cupboards, with oak used for all the internal joinery. Key pieces of loose furniture include mid-century classics by such Danish designers as Hans Wegner and Poul Kjærholm.

Another set of pocket doors separates a wing holding a den plus children's or guest accommodation, which could easily be converted into a self-contained apartment, complete with its own bathroom. Another spoke within the pin-wheel plan holds a study and the primary suite, with sliding screens used once again to create flexibility and potential privacy. In this way, Hjeltnes offers various choices about the way that the house can be used and enjoyed, while cohesion and simplicity are balanced with textural interest and subtle changes of height, volume and scale.

For Hjeltnes, other key references include the work of Jørn Utzon (see p. 88), Luis Barragán and Frank Lloyd Wright, as well as the work of Rudolph Schindler, particularly in relation to the use of the pin-wheel plan. But there is also a dialogue here between past and present, with Hjeltnes also citing Roman residences and, of course, Japan.

'I really like my architecture to be like a good book, in a way, which might be quite anonymous on the outside but adventurous on the inside,' says Hjeltnes. 'So the exteriors of this house are very calm, but the richness is on the inside, and the combination of spatial richness and tranquillity certainly attracts me. This project is very dear to my heart and I'm very happy with the spatial arrangement and the richness of possibilities, but most of all with the atmosphere of the house.'[3]

Below The kitchen is situated at the front of the house, close to the main entrance hall, and features a dining table by Kjærholm, chairs by Arne Jacobsen and a PH5 ceiling light by Poul Henningsen.

Below and right The main entrance in particular has a Japanese quality, with its echoes of a traditional genkan combined with the use of sliding screens that open up to reveal a view of the dining room and the spaces beyond.

Left The exteriors are in pale brick punctuated by lattices at key points, while the roofline extends over the entrance porch and again over the integrated terrace that sits alongside the dining room.

The dining room sits within an important axial point of the house, yet is also a welcoming space in its own right, with its dramatic angled ceiling and clerestory window drawing sunlight across the brickwork walls.

Villa S

Modern living in a garden city

The Norwegian city of Bergen, on the west coast, offers many temptations. The setting is certainly seductive and there is easy access to the fjords, the mountains and countless hiking trails. Yet the weather here is famously unpredictable and it can rain for as many as 250 days a year. When architect Todd Saunders decided to design and build a house for himself and his family here, the weather was a key consideration along with the need to respond to the site itself, situated towards the southern edge of the city in the leafy neighbourhood of Tveiterås.

'The design was partly a reaction to the weather and it does rain a lot here,' says Saunders. 'So I decided to lift the house off the ground, so that almost the entire building becomes an umbrella for the outside spaces beneath it. So, when they were younger, my daughters could go outside and use the swings under the house even when it was raining or snowing.'[1]

Canadian-born Saunders, whose office is based in Bergen and whose portfolio spans both sides of the Atlantic, settled on the garden city of Tveiterås after spotting an available site. The neighbourhood was laid out by the pioneering modernist architect Leif Grung, who also designed a number of houses here, including the family home where his son, fellow architect Geir Grung (see p. 130) grew up. The site itself is at the foot of a steeply rising and wooded hillside, forming a backdrop for the new building, which looks out onto an open garden and the views beyond.

Saunders decided to stretch the new house lengthways on the site, maximizing the sense of connection with the landscape while creating a choice of outdoor rooms and terraces. The main body of the steel-framed, spruce-clad house has been elevated with a combination of slim structural pillars plus a clean line of storage units that sit alongside the integrated carport at one end of the house, while the main entrance is located towards the centre of the plan. This engaging 'promenade architecturale' offers a heightened sense of anticipation and expectation on the short journey towards the front door, which is also sheltered from the elements by the floating house above.

The entrance sequence on the ground-floor level fuses practicality with this curated sense of arrival. Coat cupboards, a restroom and den sit to one side of the spacious entry hallway, while a suspended staircase – made of plywood and fibreglass – offers a clear invitation to climb upwards to the main level of the house.

Here, the key living spaces and bedrooms benefit from their elevated position, both in terms of the quality of the light and the open views. A large family kitchen and dining area are positioned at the centre of the plan, while a service core holding the bathroom and utility room helps to lightly separate the sitting room at the far end of the house; this, in turn, leads out to a spacious but sheltered balcony, protected by the projecting roofline. Two children's bedrooms are at the rear, while the primary suite sits at the opposite end of the house, consisting of a dressing room, bathroom and bedroom with access to another integrated terrace.

The interiors, developed in collaboration with Swedish artist and designer Hannes Wingate, fuse bespoke elements, contemporary furniture and vintage pieces. Storage is threaded in throughout, while a number of traditional ingredients – such as the wood-burning fireplace in the sitting room – have been interpreted in a contemporary manner. Modest splashes of colour stand out against the pale, natural palette of materials inside, contrasting with the dark coating of the timber cladding on the outside, which accentuates the sculptural outline of the building.

At the summit of the house, Saunders decided to create a space for himself: a generously scaled study and library, which leads out onto a roof terrace. This engaging space, in particular, has something of a treehouse quality, raised up among the branches of the neighbouring trees. 'With my clients I have noticed that they work hard and when it comes to the design of their home they like to have something that is a gift to themselves. That is often a nice bedroom, or a special bathroom, but for me the library is

The design of the house offers a choice of sheltered terraces and decks that can be used at almost any time of year, while offering natural extensions of the living spaces within.

Todd Saunders

Bergen
Norway

2014

my gift to myself. Books are really a part of me and I'm not that interested in television, so the library was a space somewhere between a want and a need.'[2]

In this respect and many others, Villa S serves as a laboratory of ideas for Saunders. Yet at the same time the house offers a clear, almost graphic composition and a very ordered layout, with much of daily, family living arranged on the one principal level. This translates into a very ordered, functional house, as well as a home that is welcoming, layered and characterful.

'The house has given me a framework for my life and has really been a kind of refuge for me over the last few years,' says Saunders. 'It's so important to come home to a place where you can be by your hearth and lay your head down, but that also fits in with all of your needs. That's what this house has done and it has made my life a lot easier in a very practical sense. It has given so much more than I ever expected and become a place to create memories. It keeps on giving back to me. It has given me much more confidence in what I do and I'd actually like to do a couple more over my lifetime. This won't be my last house for myself, I can guarantee that.'[3]

Opposite and left The dark timber cladding accentuates the outline of the house against the backdrop of the rising hillside beyond, while mature trees soften the garden setting.

‘There’s no excuse not to go outside and, for me, I can go and fix my bike or set up my camping gear and not worry about the rain. The whole house became a kind of tent sheltering these fresh-air spaces.’

Opposite and above
The ground-floor entrance hallway houses the staircase that leads up to the principal living spaces at mid-level, including the combined kitchen and dining room at the centre of the plan.

1%

Opposite and right
A spinal circulation route connects the key spaces on the piano nobile, including the dining room and the nearby sitting room, where fitted and loose seating has been arranged around the integrated fireplace.

TOP ONE
KLIMT
VILLAS
BAUHAUS

Opposite The library/studio sits at the top of the building, providing a quiet escape with open views in one direction and glimpses of the treetops on the hillside in the other.

Left The double staircase, seen here from the kitchen/dining room, offers a sculptural element in itself, with its open treads allowing light to circulate.

Manshausen Sea Cabins

An Arctic wonderland

It was the beauty of the Arctic landscape that first drew Norwegian polar explorer Børge Ousland to the island of Manshausen. Ousland made his first solo trips to the North Pole during the 1990s, with further expeditions to the North and South Poles over subsequent years, balanced with writing and film-making. When Ousland started thinking about finding a retreat in northern Norway he was drawn to Manshausen, around an hour from the town of Bødo along the coast via the passenger ferry to Nordskot and then a short boat transfer.

'I wanted a cabin that was not too far from the airport, and so I bought Manshausen initially for personal enjoyment,' says Ousland. 'It was the beauty of nature and the surrounding landscape that fascinated me most. Engaging in outdoor activities has always been my greatest passion, be it kayaking, diving, fishing or exploring mountainous terrain. When I came to this area it was all here – a plate full of adventure and exploration. But then, after a couple of years, the idea of developing Manshausen as a resort gradually grew on me.'[1]

Ousland realized that there was potential to be unlocked, along with the opportunity to share the Arctic beauty with others. He turned to architect Snorre Stinessen to help develop a plan for the resort, which has grown gradually but considerately over time, with an emphasis on sustainability and preserving the unique setting threaded through every stage. The communal amenities at Manshausen include a restaurant and library situated in an updated farmhouse, as well as a sauna, meeting room and kayak shed. Yet it is the seven sea cabins, each named after an Arctic region, that provide the private escapes, with each offering a personal refuge focused on a key vista. Most of the cabins sit on the old stone quays, projecting out over the water.

'The most important factors for the location of the cabins were minimizing their impact on a fragile landscape while also utilizing the existing built structures on the island,' says Stinessen. 'The quays are the only remaining trace of a fairly large wooden warehouse that once stood on the island, dating back to when the waterways were the main communication line along northern Norway. Utilizing the foundations felt natural in that it preserves and enhances the historical context and the landscape. But we also wanted to offer guests privacy, while exposing them, to the elements and the views, so we chose to give priority to the individual qualities of each cabin.'[2]

The cabins were carefully positioned to ensure that the walls of floor-to-ceiling glass at the end of each one, framing the open vistas of the water and the mountains, never intrude on the sight lines of their neighbours. Each one offers both a sense of seclusion and a feeling of immersion in the natural world. Accessed from the rear, the timber-framed cabins have the quality of berthed boats with space-saving measures woven throughout. The entrance hall leads past a bunkroom and bathroom, as well as a galley kitchenette, to an open-plan lounge and the adjoining primary bedroom, both enjoying the sensitively directed views of the surroundings.

'The idea of small wooden buildings in close connection with the sea is a trademark of the area and the nearby Lofoten archipelago in particular,' Stinessen says. 'Our design is, of course, for a different time and serves a completely different function, so the inspiration of the traditional *rorbu* – or fishermen's houses – is not easily detected. Some of the design features and points of inspiration are probably linked to even older traditions in terms of how we have organized the covered porch and entrance, the natural ventilation of the buildings and the organization of the rooms.'[3]

The conscious decision to create a collection of modestly scaled buildings, rather than a traditional hotel, feels very much in keeping with the ethos of sustainability and the wish to protect the landscape. The pleasures and pursuits are also very much focused on the natural beauty of the setting: kayaking, hiking, fishing and sea eagle safaris.

'Manshausen should be a place where you can recharge,' says Ousland. 'And stepping into the sea cabins gives you this sensation of being outside in nature while being cocooned in warmth and comfort. Crafting this elusive but essential luxury was the challenge that we managed to meet and it's this achievement that brings me the greatest satisfaction.'[4]

The cabins at Manshausen are carefully positioned by the water's edge, with each one oriented towards open views of the coastal setting while also preserving the sense of seclusion and privacy for the occupants of each individual retreat.

Snorre Stinessen

Manshausen Island
Norway

2015

‘The idea of small wooden buildings in close connection with the sea is a trademark of the area and the nearby Lofoten archipelago in particular.’

Opposite and right
The interiors of the cabins are compact but intelligently and elegantly designed, making the most of the projecting picture windows, which offer a lens upon the landscape.

Above and opposite
Aluminium coats help the timber-framed cabins cope with all seasons, while they are designed to sit as lightly upon the coastline as possible, with minimal impact upon this sensitive natural environment.

Opposite One of the greatest pleasures on Manshausen is taking the time to appreciate the natural world around you, with each cabin serving as a seductive belvedere.

Above Each cabin is named after an Arctic explorer and adventurer, with the overhanging porch providing a semi-sheltered terrace.

Krokholmen House

An escape on the outer archipelago

There are thousands of islands in the Stockholm Archipelago, which spreads out for miles from the Swedish mainland. Some are accessible by roadways and bridges, some by ferries and others only by smaller boats, while countless smaller islands and outcrops remain uninhabited. The island of Krokholmen sits on the outer edges of the archipelago, offering a peaceful and sublime retreat, with an open vista eastwards to the famous lighthouse of Almagrundet in the far distance. It is an extraordinary setting in which to build a home, as Gunilla and Tomas Hoffman discovered when they first visited the island.

'We know the archipelago quite well and we had heard about this place and that there was a property for sale,' says Tomas, 'so we took the boat and had a look. What really impressed us was the location and the scenery – it was a very good location. There were two old houses here, but we could see the potential and what we might do.'[1]

The Hoffmans bought the site, right next to the shore, in 2009. It came with a hunting lodge dating from the 1940s plus a separate sauna, which had been added more recently, as well as a dock. The Hoffmans, who also have a home in the city of Stockholm itself, initially used the existing summer cottage while they thought about plans for the future. The island has electricity, but the cottage had no fresh-water source, so the family had to bring water canisters with them on the boat, which was one of the factors that led them towards an entirely new building.

The couple had already noted contemporary houses on the archipelago designed by Tham & Videgård, including a summer retreat on the island of Husarö, which they spotted on a boat trip. They approached architects Bolle Tham and Martin Videgård and asked them to design a new residence to replace the 1940s cottage.

'The remote site, on the outskirts of the archipelago, is quite unique since it's extremely close to the waterfront,' says Videgård. 'You have a very direct relationship to the horizon, with the sun reflecting in the water, and a direct relation to the elements. What pleased us about the project was the realization of the idea to create an almost temporary shelter – a tent-like space in nature.'[2]

The expressive, sculptural roofline became one of the defining elements of the project. Made with glulam wooden beams coated in zinc, the high tent shelters the open-plan living area at the front of the house, which also features a wall of sliding glass to the front framing the open views across the water. Sitting on a smooth concrete pad, this generously scaled and enticing space hosts the lounge, dining area and kitchen, while a semi-sheltered terrace sits to one side. The principal suite and a guest room are positioned to the rear, as well as a bathroom served by water from a new desalination plant installed in a shed nearby. The interiors have a warm, organic quality throughout, with ash for the ceilings and walls, teak for the window frames and larch cladding for the exteriors.

Some years later, the Hoffmans – who have three grown-up children – decided that they needed more space. This time, they replaced the sauna with a larger building, also designed by Tham & Videgård, which holds guest accommodation as well as a sauna, with an open-sided terrace, or porch, positioned at the centre. Rather than bringing in every ingredient piece by piece, as was the case the first time around, the architects opted for a prefabricated construction system for the new, linear guest cabin, with units delivered to site for rapid assembly and completed in 2022. Although different in composition and form, these two buildings do share similar materials and have established a dialogue with one another. More than this, the guest lodge adds another layer of possibility within this escapist setting, which the family now use not only in the summer months, but also at various other times of the year, including the winter.

'We love the sense of privacy here,' says Gunilla Hoffman. 'It is very quiet, but we see sea eagles, the elk that swim from island to island, seals and foxes – so many animals and birds. We do have to make a plan before we come to Krokholmen and bring everything we need, but we still have five good restaurants fifteen or twenty minutes away by boat. It is a great combination.'[3]

The curvaceous, tent-like roof canopy forms one of the most distinctive features of the principal residence, which sits close to the water's edge but is softened by its backdrop of mature trees.

Above and opposite
The kitchen, dining area and lounge are held within an open-plan living area at the front of the house, where a sliding wall of glass retracts to create an easy transition to the adjoining terrace, while framing an open vista of the archipelago.

Left and opposite High timber ceilings, timber-panelled walls and extensive joinery lend the house a highly crafted and organic character, while concrete floors offer a practical surface for island life.

Left The main residence is now complemented by a more recent addition: a guest lodge that also holds a sauna and other amenities.

Opposite below and above
Bespoke, fitted elements such as the kitchen, island and integrated storage lend the interiors of the house a pleasing sense of cohesion, while the adjoining terrace offers a partially sheltered outdoor room suitable for summer dining.

Villa Birkedal

A house among the trees

Jan Henrik Jansen

Møn
Denmark

2016

'Here, every space is a cylinder, so I started by designing each room as a round space, taking that as the starting point, and asking how a circular living room or bedroom might be arranged.'

The Danish word *birkedal* translates as 'birch valley'. It is certainly an apt name for a house, designed and built by architect Jan Henrik Jansen, which is not only bordered by a grove of silver birch trees but one that is also distinctly organic in its character. Consisting of a collection of intersecting, timber-clad cylinders, it is a unique home, immersed in nature and standing close to the coastline on the picturesque Danish island of Møn.

'"Birkedal" is also my wife's second name, so that's why we chose it, as well as having the birch trees here,' says Jansen, who was born in Germany but has lived and worked in Denmark ever since he was an architecture student. 'I like to think that I used three materials on the outside of the house – spruce trunks for the cladding, Cor-Ten steel for the windows but also the birch trees, because when you see their white trunks alongside Villa Birkedal, they are so significant and such an important part of the context. For me, it was all about materials that fit into the colours of nature and how they weather over time.'[1]

For Jansen, whose practice is based near Copenhagen, Villa Birkedal was the third in a sequence of self-build projects on the island of Møn, which is around a two-and-a-half-hour drive southwards from the Danish capital. Each of these projects was purposefully very different in character, providing a new challenge and a fresh learning curve in each case. The predecessor to Villa Birkedal sits right next door, sharing the same leafy site, yet has a distinctly different personality and a linear outline.

'This house was, in a way, an exercise,' says Jansen of Villa Birkedal, 'and a chance to explore another architectural language, another composition and another way of designing a house. Here, every space is a cylinder, so I started by designing each room as a round space, taking that as the starting point, and asking how a circular living room or bedroom might be arranged, and so on. Multiple ideas then developed before I started working on the final composition.'[2]

The final form of the house was also influenced by the site, which was initially home to a garden allotment and a small shed. Jansen chose to place the building on a gently raised bluff on the northern boundary, looking out over fields and forests, while the southern approach runs through a garden set within a clearing in the birch woods, complete with a circular sauna and garden room that formed a prototype for the house itself. Another key

Consisting of a series of cylinders coated in slender spruce trunks, Villa Birkedal has a highly organic character, blending into its rural setting.

The lens-like picture windows on the bedroom cylinders and the main living spaces are largely focused on open views across the fields, while the surrounding trees form a natural, protective backdrop.

point of inspiration was the arrival of the first of Jansen's two children not long before he started work on the house, which influenced the evolution of what then became a true family retreat, with the architect trying to look at the project from a child's point of view.

The construction process began in 2011 and took five years to complete, with Jansen balancing Villa Birkedal with other commissions as well as his growing family commitments. The architect would travel down to Møn for three days a week, working on the construction of the house himself, including the groundwork and building the circular plywood frames into which he poured concrete for the foundations. The interconnecting timber-framed spaces were then placed on these cement pads, along with insulation and panelling, before being coated in spruce trunks positioned vertically on the drums and punctuated with the Cor-Ten window frames, which have rusted naturally to an earthy-brown hue.

Inside, Jansen opted for a calm, cohesive palette of materials. The collection of circular cocoons is tied together by the use of pale, rounded beach pebbles set into the floors, while the bespoke wooden wall panelling – with its integrated storage cupboards and other ingredients – is painted a soothing white. From the porch, the entrance hall leads to two of the bedrooms and a bathroom within one wing of the building, while the other holds the combined kitchen and dining room towards the centre of the plan, with the sitting room beyond, plus the principal bedroom and separate bathroom.

Jansen also designed much of the bespoke oak furniture, while opting for brass lighting and fittings, which work well with the organic character of the other carefully chosen materials. Picture windows are largely oriented towards the vista across the open farmland, while the bedrooms have framed views of the trees. Terraces around the villa offer outdoor rooms within a rural retreat that Jansen and his family tend to use over the summer, while renting the villa for the rest of the year through the Holiday Architecture (or 'Urlaubs Arkitektur') collective. With the combination of the setting and the organic quality of the materials, the villa has a truly escapist character.

'I was interested in creating a quiet mood with natural materials that patinate and have their own character and texture,' says Jansen. 'But it was also important to me to make sure that you would be able to feel the significance of the shapes of these spaces that wrap around you. I sometimes think, especially in the smaller rooms, that it feels not like being in a space but being in a cocoon, with this idea of being embraced and protected. All of this is related to these gentle, round shapes.'[3]

Opposite and left A unifying palette of materials – timber panelling with raised batons for the walls and integrated storage, rounded pebbles for the floors, and brass for such elements as the kitchen and lighting – creates a soothing sense of cohesion throughout.

Above An additional cylinder holds the entrance porch to the house, as seen from the garden, while a terrace alongside also sits on a round footprint.

Above and left Bedrooms and bathrooms adopt a similar palette of materials to the main living spaces, while the beds themselves are positioned so that they face key views framed by the projecting picture windows.

Fleinvær Refugium

A mesmerizing Nordland retreat

Fleinvær Refugium, on the Nordland coast of Norway, is a house of many rooms. By the water, musician and composer Håvard Lund has created a micro village, overlooking an archipelago of around 360 small islands, one for each day of the year. The Refugium has grown over the years, under a master plan sketched out by architect Sami Rintala, to include a collection of small sleeping huts alongside a meeting house, a studio and a contemplation room, as well as – most importantly – a communal sauna. This organic approach seems very much in keeping with the history of a small community, accessible only by boat, which evolved over the centuries through subsistence farming and fishing.

'In the beginning, there might have been an idea to create one bigger building with all these different functions in one place,' says Rintala, who has an office and a family home in the city of Bodø, around one hour away by passenger ferry, as well as a second office in Oslo. 'But then we began to think differently. Now you see that all the buildings are divided into these different parts of the household and then the main building, or meeting house. What happens then is that you have free space between them, and even when the wind is blowing, you will always find a sheltered lee space in these small pockets and the spaces in between. It helps to create a microclimate, especially when the sun starts shining.'[1]

The project began in around 2004, when Lund visited some friends nearby and was captured by the remote Arctic location. There are no cars or shops, but there are sea eagles, seals and passing whales, as well as an extraordinary coastal landscape. He began thinking about a retreat that could be shared by visiting artists as well as paying guests, leading to conversations with the local farmer about acquiring land for the Refugium.

'Fleinvær got to me from the first moment,' says Lund, who now balances running the Refugium with his work as a musician and musical director. 'Initially, it was meant as a workplace for myself, but as time went on, I felt a need to share what I had found at Fleinvær with others. I wanted to create a workplace unlike anything else in the world. I gain energy from other people being here and working. We have musicians, artists, photographers and choreographers. But the nicest thing to do is to mix people, so in that way, I am a curator.'[2]

The first building completed at Fleinvær was the sauna, which sits on a redundant pontoon that became available after a new pier was built to serve the ferry. Beyond this, Rintala sketched out a master plan for the Refugium, drawing inspiration from the small coastal villages and traditional farmsteads. A close collaboration began not only with Lund but also with colleagues at Tyin Tegnestue, with contributions from visiting architectural students from Trondheim University, who helped to construct elements of the Refugium as part of their work-experience programme.

The meeting house was a key element of the project, holding the communal kitchen and dining room, where guests come together to cook, eat and talk. A studio sits alongside the meeting house on the hillside, offering a spacious, open room for rehearsals, recitals or readings. Further up the hill, there is a floating meditation room, or 'room of reflection', perched upon a single steel stem, with open views across the surrounding islands and a design partly inspired by the example of the 'njalla' – a traditional storehouse used by the Sami people in northern Norway and Finland.

The small wooden sleeping cabins were prefabricated and then brought in by helicopter, with each one anchored to the hillside and carefully placed for the views and for privacy. There is also a bathhouse alongside the sauna and a utility room, while Lund's own private home is also situated alongside the shore. In this way, the Refugium grew over a number of years, with the majority of the 'house' completed by 2017.

'The local municipality was very friendly to the project and they allowed us to move at our pace and accepted the plan as a whole, especially after we proved that we could actually build it,' says Rintala. 'The scale of the "village" and the placing of each unit in the landscape communicates with the traditional way of building on these islands and this way one can regulate which units are being warmed based on the number of visitors, controlling the use of energy.'[3]

The elevated meditation room, on its steel stem, frames a view of the coast (see p. 227), while the two matching cabins a little further down the hillside hold a multipurpose studio and a meeting room that includes a communal kitchen and dining room.

Rintala Eggertsson
& Tyin Tegnestue

Fleinvær
Norway

2017

Given the remote and precious setting, sustainability has been threaded through the entire project and the design programme. Rintala has remained intimately involved in the project, visiting regularly not only to help with the building programme but also to enjoy time here fishing and cooking. The latest additions to Fleinvær are a greenhouse and a small performance pavilion, which could be the last of the Refugium's many rooms.

'Of course, when you have a project on the other side of the world, you don't see so much of it after it's finished,' says Rintala. 'But here, the great thing is that I am almost living next to it, as I can be here in an hour, so I have to take responsibility and help Håvard keep the place going, and it's always such a nice place to come to. Sometimes I don't come to work but just to fish, be in nature and be with friends. And if I have guests from abroad who want to see the archipelago, this is the best place to come and makes a very good base camp.'[4]

Above and oppoiste
The twin cabins and the terrace between them form the most sociable spaces at Fleinvær, incorporating a spacious dining and meeting area overlooking the hamlet and towards the small islands spread out along the coast.

Below The floating meditation room can also be used as an additional sleeping cabin, offering a captivating vista of the coastal landscape.

Left and below The sleeping cabins are modestly scaled escape pods, with desks and sleeping platforms. Guests are encouraged to gather at the meeting house, the studio or the sauna for more social experiences.

Given the remote and precious setting, sustainability has been threaded through the entire project and the design programme.

Fanø Summer House

A Danish island haven

Knud Holscher & Tollgard Studio

Fanø
Denmark

2018

A gentle line of dunes sits between the house and the beach, offering a welcome degree of privacy while helping to shelter the single-storey home from sea breezes.

The Danish island of Fanø, alongside the country's western coast, is a place of many delights. Accessible only by ferry, Fanø is a coastal retreat with a slower pace of living, where cycling is the favoured mode of transport and the beaches are wide and open. The island landscape, the big skies and the open vistas across the water are the great attractions here, along with the birds and wildlife, the coastal cuisine and other similar quiet pleasures. The small villages and hamlets certainly have an alluring feel to them, drawing in settlers who have fallen in love with the island's unique character.

Such was the case with the owners of the Fanø Summer House, designed by the celebrated Danish modernist architect Knud Holscher and designer Staffan Tollgård. The creative collaboration between the client and the design team resulted in a beachside home that makes the most of these connections to the natural world and the coastal surroundings while offering a family home that is sophisticated in its design and detailing but also suitably informal and relaxed.

'We wanted our Danish haven to be peaceful and nestled in nature,' say Holscher and Tollgård's clients, who spend much of the year living in the city. 'Fanø is a place for recharging together, so we wanted a home that was unmistakably a Danish summer house. At the same time, we wanted the design to be bold and balance both form and function. Finally, we wanted to prioritize how it felt to experience the house from the inside, rather than focus on the outward aesthetic.'[1]

For the owners of the Fanø Summer House, the island was reminiscent of childhood summers spent on another Danish island on the western coast of Jutland. Back in 2007, the family bought a small cottage here, spending vacations with their young children in a traditional island retreat dating from the 1970s. But over time two small children became three teenagers, with an energetic dog also taking up residence, leading to a rethink and plans for a larger, more substantial home fully tailored to the needs of the family.

They decided to approach Holscher, an architect and industrial designer who began his career working with Arne Jacobsen (see p. 48), including two years spent in England during the early 1960s working as a project architect on Jacobsen's St Catherine's College in Oxford. Having been a partner at Krohn & Hartvig Rasmussen Architects for many years, Holscher opened his own studio during the 1990s, with a range of projects that has included cultural and residential commissions, as well as his own vacation cabin on a peninsula in northwest Zealand. For the interiors, they turned to London-based, Swedish-born designer Staffan Tollgård.

'Knud Holscher is one of the world's greatest architects, so we were privileged that he agreed to work with us on this project,' say his clients. 'As for Staffan Tollgård, we had worked together in the past and he knows our family extremely well. One of our dreams was to design custom furniture to suit the unusual layout of the house. As a Swede, Staffan was born into the Scandinavian aesthetic and was able to carry this throughout the project.'[2]

The new, single-storey house faces the dunes and the sea beyond. A dynamic, wing-like roof, made of coated plywood, forms a characterful canopy over the cabin, which features an expansive living room with floor-to-ceiling walls of glass connecting with the adjoining terrace and the landscape itself. This great room is gently zoned with a dining area at one end, where the table doubles as a table-tennis court, and then a generous lounge at the other, while a double-sided fireplace offers a light sense of separation between the two.

The kitchen, bedrooms, bathrooms and entrance hall all sit within a neat row towards the rear of the house, which extends outwards at either end to help enhance the sense of privacy and enclosure for the more open-plan living spaces, as well as the outdoor spaces around them. The layout creates an ordered and pleasing degree of separation between the social family zones and the more private realm of the home, with each member of the family granted their own escape pod.

Natural materials and colour tones predominate, with stone flag floors providing cohesion and a long timber-panelled wall offering a neat demarcation line between the two key parts of the cabin. Much of the furniture is bespoke, some designed by Tollgård and some designed and made by Københavns Møbelsnedkeri, again making extensive use of organic materials such as smoked oak. There are also one or two mid-century touches, such as the CH25 rattan chairs designed by Hans Wegner. Importantly, the considered assembly of colours and textures never overwhelms the dune landscape that is a constant presence, framed by the walls of glass around the great room.

'We designed the summer house to bring everyone together,' say the owners of the Fanø Summer House, 'and the main living room is a modern interpretation of a Viking hall. The central glass wall is designed to slide open so that we can bring the outside in on warm days, and the colour palette is entirely composed of colours that can be found in nature, which makes the house blend beautifully into its surroundings.

'We love having friends and family over and cooking, as well as going for long walks with our dog in the dunes or on the beach. From the windows, we have an endless procession of wildlife – the migratory birds, rabbits, hares, foxes, pheasants and deer. It's all about slowing down and just being in nature.'[3]

Below Walls of floor-to-ceiling glass connect the living space with the surrounding dunes, while also leading out to a choice of outdoor rooms and terraces. The sofa is by Living Divani.

Opposite The open-plan living room, with a lounge at one end and a dining area at the other, is protected by its curvaceous plywood ceilings. The bespoke dining table, chairs and cabinet were made by Københavns Møbelsnedkeri.

Opposite The kitchen, bedrooms and bathrooms sit beyond the dark timber of the central dividing wall, which defines the 'public' and private realms of the house.

Right The overhanging roof canopy helps to protect the house in winter and provide shade during the summer, while also sheltering part of the deck that borders the building.

Opposite and below
The wing-like roof canopy is the most dramatic feature of the house, providing a dynamic, sculptural element but also helping to define the main living area and demarcate this open-plan space from the rest of the building.

Villa Sagalid

A shimmering cubist composition

Perched on a cliff overlooking the waters of the Stockholm Archipelago, Villa Sagalid provides a striking, sculptural presence within the coastal landscape. The layered, cubist composition is certainly eye-catching in itself, but so too is the ceramic coating of the building. Composed of a collection of hand-crafted, glazed tiles hanging on the surface of the concrete-framed structure, these ceramic plates shimmer and shine according to the changing light and the direction of the sun. In doing so, they help to bring this family retreat to life.

'There are a lot of pine trees on the plot, so my idea was that the ceramics would look a bit like the bark on the trees, but enlarged,' says architect Thomas Sandell, of Stockholm-based Sandell Sandberg. 'The plate itself is dark brown, but there is a bit of blue in it, which we added to pick up the sky light. It was a great success. In addition to being very stylish, it blends well with the surroundings.'

The house is one of a series of retreats that Sandell has designed and built on the islands of the Stockholm Archipelago, including a summer house for himself and his family. Villa Sagalid was commissioned by a couple with young children, who had acquired the mesmerizing site on the island of Djurö, which is situated close to the mainland and accessible by car via a sequence of bridges that eventually connect back to the city itself. The parcel of land, also accessible by boat, came with an existing summer cottage that had replaced a much older building that had been destroyed in a fire. Yet it was the landscape itself, with its mature trees and the elevated position on the cliffs, looking out over the coastline, that primarily attracted the family and their architect.

Sandell and his clients opted to replace the cottage with a new and bespoke family residence, but one that was fully aligned with the rugged, shifting topography of the setting and respected the existing pine trees, which were carefully protected and preserved. The house is arranged on four levels, while the building has been pushed into the hillside in such a way that the ground floor connects with the deck and pool terrace facing the water, while the floor above flows out onto another generous terrace to one side of the home, where there is another choice of outdoor rooms.

The plan of the house presents a welcome degree of flexibility in terms of the way that the family chooses to use the building at various times of the year. During the summer, in particular, the sliding glass doors between the combined kitchen and dining area open up to offer a fluid connection between the interiors and exteriors. The principal level above holds the sitting room, library and a music room, also known as the 'winter room', as well as a guest suite. Family bedrooms are located on level three, while an elevated sky lounge stands at the summit of the building, giving a treehouse feel with its open vista of the archipelago. As well as the stairway, a lift ties all of these floors together.

There are constant connections to the surroundings throughout, via picture windows and the provision of porches and hinterland spaces between indoors and out. The interiors are lifted by shifts in height and volume, while the choice of materials and furnishings offers a warm and welcoming foundation for family living. Sandell also created a guest house and a timber-framed, glass-sided yoga pavilion nearby, which adds to the rich choice of escapist spaces.

The bespoke ceramic tiles for the exterior, crafted by Koninklijke Tichelaar in Makkum, the Netherlands, and partly inspired by the work of Alvar Aalto, add to the unique personality of Villa Sagalid and have become one of its defining elements. 'The strength of ceramics is that you can create your own shapes and patterns,' says Sandell. 'The house is exposed to the weather and up on a hill, so it must be able to withstand the water and wind, so the ceramic fits well, because it is a very durable material. There is every possibility to shape it into something unique.'

The multilayered house sits on the clifftop, with terraces and a pool deck among the rocks in front of the building, and steps leading down to a boat dock and the sea.

Opposite The building is coated in dark ceramic tiles that shimmer in the sunlight and vary in tone according to the seasons and the time of day, lending the house a dynamic character.

Above The house and its adjoining terraces, as well as the infinity pool, offer views across the islands of the archipelago and the gentle waterborne traffic that helps to connect them together.

Above and left The interiors of the building, along with the integrated terraces and roof decks, are carefully positioned to take advantage of key views across the archipelago.

Above This multipurpose entertaining space is positioned on the top floor of the house, while a roof terrace is located directly alongside it. For dining, an elevator helps connect the space with the kitchen on the lower-ground floor.

Opposite The double-height dining area alongside the kitchen offers a dramatic focal point for family meal times and gatherings, enjoying open views from the table and connections with the adjoining terrace.

Above and left Mid-level living spaces and family bedrooms savour framed vistas of the coastal surroundings, with the careful planning of the house ensuring that all key areas feature picture windows and connections to the archipelago.

PAN Cabin Three

Floating above the forest

Within farming families, each and every generation likes to make its own mark in one way or another. This was very much the case for Kristian Rostad, who grew up on the family farm in southeastern Norway, and his wife, Christine Mowinckel. Their dramatic addition to the farmstead was a triptych of A-framed cabins floating high among the treetops in the forests of Finnskogen. Designed by architect Espen Surnevik, the eye-catching PAN Cabins have brought ecotourism to the woods and the opportunity to immerse oneself in nature within the most peaceful of settings.

'My father was into grains and potatoes, as well as working in forestry in the winter, selling wood for construction and materials,' says Rostad. 'It is still a working farm but there have been some major changes and we thought of doing something different. We started thinking about what we should be doing for the future and we ended up with these three cabins.'[1]

Rostad's first career was in journalism, working for the Norwegian Broadcasting Corporation, or NRK. His wife Christine, who he met while they were both living in Oslo, worked in theatre for many years and has continued teaching drama even after making the move to Finnskogen. The couple were already thinking about life beyond Oslo when Rostad was offered a redundancy package by NRK and the chance to return home to the farmstead.

'I'm from Molde, on the Norwegian fjords, and so I was not that familiar with this area,' says Mowinckel. 'I didn't realize how beautiful it was before I came here and when we decided to do something with our own footprint we thought about opening it up and inviting people to stay here in the forest. But to do that we needed a place for people to stay. So we contacted Espen Surnevik.'[2]

Based in Oslo, Surnevik and his practice have developed a portfolio of highly contextual projects rooted in the Norwegian landscape and a respect for the Nordic vernacular. Rostad and Mowinckel already knew his work, particularly his church in the nearby town of Våler: a contemporary sacred space designed and built to replace a former house of worship destroyed in a fire.

'Våler Church is around a forty-minute drive away from us and it is really spectacular,' says Mowinckel. 'Espen is very adventurous and we thought the church was so interesting architecturally.'[3]

'And also made of wood, which was not so common for a church at that time,' Rostad explains. 'It was very inspirational for us and, since we had this project in the forest, we wanted to be able to use wood as one of our main materials.'[4]

The experience of working on Våler Church was helpful in terms of Surnevik's knowledge of the local area and its artisans. More than this, the couple found Surnevik to be a good listener and responsive to their proposals for a forest retreat. Initially, the architect and client considered the idea of a set of modern treehouses fixed to the trees themselves, but over time, ideas developed for a triptych of self-supporting tower houses.

'When we first looked at building treehouses, we realized that it was not such a good solution for the trees,' says Surnevik. 'So we ended up with a separate steel-framed structure to lift them from the ground and, of course, it creates a surprising and unusual experience to visit the cabins when they are lifted up in the forest. The most important part of it for me was the special atmosphere that this creates – being secure in this elevated cabin.'[5]

One of the most challenging elements of the process was to design the strong but lightweight steel framework to support the cabins without distracting from the purity of the floating, A-framed residences themselves. Eventually, Surnevik opted for separate spiral staircases to gain entry, contained in steel-mesh cylinders, with a bridge linking them to the cabins while enhancing the overall composition.

Inside, PAN Cabin Three – like its companions nearby – makes the most of all available space while adopting a palette of pine, Douglas fir and oak. Both ends of the cabin are encased in a double-height pyramid of glass, framing the forest views. At one end, a lounge is arranged around a wood-burning stove, while, at the opposite end, a dining area and galley kitchen are found. Between

Access to the elevated cabin is provided by a spiral staircase within the ancillary tower alongside, while the sky bridge connects with the residence itself.

Espen Surnevik

Åsnes
Norway

2018

PAN Cabin Three

these spaces, towards the centre, there is a compact service core – holding bathrooms and storage space – with a mezzanine above containing the bedroom. The design ensures that views over the forest can be fully enjoyed even from the sleeping platform, adding to the sense of total immersion in the tree canopy.

'It is an absolutely unique project, which belongs to the site, the forest and the landscape,' says Surnevik, who has enjoyed spending time at the cabins himself. 'It's always strange to be in a building you have developed with great intellectual intensity over the years, but the finest thing about the small, elevated PAN Cabins is that safe feeling of being inside these warm, wooden interiors, where you are all alone with the dark forest. I really like that intention and feeling.'[6]

Each of the three cabins is carefully positioned to make the most of this feeling of tranquillity, as well as maximizing privacy for the inhabitants of each one. For Rostad and Mowinckel, one of the most satisfying aspects of the project is how the cabins and their surroundings take on a different character over the course of the four seasons. Like sophisticated bird hides or lookout posts, they present an extraordinary stage for viewing the wildlife of the forest all year round. But during the winter especially, the cabins offer a striking presence in the forest, when cross-country skiing and snowshoe hiking take over from mountain biking and horse riding. In the snow months, the feeling of seclusion, escapism and warmth within PAN Three and its neighbours is mesmerizing.

'If you like architecture and you like nature, then it's a very good combination,' says Mowinckel. 'There is something very special about coming up to this height and looking out into the trees. For me, I feel relaxed because I am in control and I can gaze out and see so much more around me. It's the feeling of being in a lookout post deep in the forest.'[7]

Above Warmed by a wood-burning stove, the lounge sits at one end of the cabin (left), looking out over the treetops, while a mezzanine sleeping platform is positioned at the centre, floating above the bathroom (above).

Opposite The compact kitchen and dining area sit at the end of the cabin, while the area towards the centre holds the main entrance hall, as well as connecting to the bathroom.

Below and right The design of the cabin makes the most of the A-framed structure, with the sleeping platform situated within the central peak (below) and the living spaces at either end making the most of the high ceilings (right).

Opposite The cabin sits within the forest, making it an extraordinary escape surrounded by nature, where quiet, calm and solitude are the great luxuries.

Jacobsen House

A Faroese hillside home

One of the most traditional forms of architecture in the Faroe Islands, as well as in some parts of Iceland, is the turf house. Early settlers made long houses and homesteads using stone and timber that were topped with grass roofs made from blocks of living turf cut from the land itself. In the twenty-first century, turf houses are being revived and reinterpreted, including distinctly modern buildings such as the family home that architect Ósbjørn Jacobsen has designed and built in the village of Syðrugøta, on the eastern coast of the Faroese island of Eysturoy.

'It's the idea of not knowing exactly where the house starts and the landscape ends,' says Jacobsen, who shares the hillside residence with his wife Sigrún and their three children. 'It was definitely a theme that I wanted to explore, with this idea of making a cut into the green blanket of the hill, lifting it and placing yourself underneath it, so that when you experience the house, it looks as though it is growing out of the landscape itself.'[1]

Jacobsen grew up in this coastal village, known for its long-established fishing industry and for being the birthplace of celebrated Faroese singer Eivør Pálsdóttir. It is one of the oldest recorded settlements on the Faroe Islands and is home to multiple generations of Jacobsen's family, including his father, who is a carpenter, and his brother, who lives close by. Although Jacobsen was born in the village and started his education in the local schools, he only returned home in 2011 after many years away.

In the Danish city of Aarhus, Jacobsen studied architecture and straight after graduation joined the well-known practice of Henning Larsen, which was founded by Larsen himself in 1959 and has been growing ever since. Initially based in Copenhagen, where he first met his Faroese partner, Jacobsen was then asked to relocate to Reykjavík to work on the design and build of the Harpa, the city's waterfront concert hall created by Henning Larsen in conjunction with Icelandic artist Olafur Eliasson. The Harpa became a seven-year project, with Jacobsen and his family living in Reykjavík full-time for four of those years. Eventually, the family decided it was time to settle back in the Faroe Islands.

'We said, okay, let's go home and that's something that we were really happy with,' says Jacobsen, who was a partner at Henning Larsen by that point. 'But also I had no intention of working on that kind of scale again and was more interested in working on smaller projects. So setting up an office here was at the back of my mind when we moved here, and then it began to grow organically.'[2]

After some time shuttling between the Faroe Islands and Copenhagen, Jacobsen and the practice began winning architectural competitions and commissions at home. Eventually, Jacobsen opened a dedicated Henning Larsen office in Syðrugøta, which has grown into a team of fourteen people. A number of their key projects have explored the relationship between architecture and landscape, as seen in their Eystur Town Hall in the neighbouring village of Norðragøta, where the building spans the River Eiðis and its grass roof appears to carry the green river banks over the water.

Jacobsen's family house similarly forges an intimate connection with the surroundings while its sculptural roofline echoes the shape of the mountains across the bay. The entire building has been gently pushed into the hillside, with black timber cladding contrasting with the turf roof, which needs a trim just twice a year, a service sometimes provided by the sheep that graze in the neighbouring pasture.

The house is accessed from the roadway to the rear, where a set of steps alongside the integrated garage lead down to the entrance to the principal storey. Here, a generous central hall separates bedrooms and bathrooms to either side while carrying on naturally towards the living area and an open vista of the fjord, framed by banks of picture windows. This fluid, open-plan living space spans the entire width of the house, with the sitting room to one side and the dining area and kitchen to the other, supplemented by a semi-sheltered balcony alongside looking across the fields and hills.

Oak floors unify this space, while reconstituted timber boards line the ceiling, enhancing the warm, organic character of the interiors. Insulation and glazing are

The house offers a modern interpretation of the traditional turf house, with the pasture carrying over the roof of the building like a green blanket, while the angular geometry seems to echo the mountain peaks in the distance.

Ósbjørn Jacobsen

Syðrugøta
Faroe Islands

2019

Opposite and below
Seen from the grazing pasture alongside the house, the building takes on a different character, with the combination of a cantilevered deck alongside the dining room and the characterful timber-clad elevations accentuating the contemporary quality of the architecture. The main entrance, meanwhile, steps down from the driveway and the access road to the rear.

high specification, by necessity, while the underfloor heating is fed by a ground-source heat pump. This part of the house cantilevers outwards over an undercroft, which holds services and a self-contained apartment. From the house, the views encompass the village spread out along the shoreline and a dramatic natural panorama.

'As an architect, it is really interesting to draw something for yourself,' says Jacobsen, who worked on the construction of the house himself, along with his father and brother, as a self-build project. 'It's a learning process and I can see that I have used this project as a reference in other work, especially of course when it's housing. This is a special environment and in the Faroe Islands we do have this strong tradition of building, where you really involve yourself in the project. The single-family houses that we have done, including this one, have become a huge influence on my work.'[3]

Left The cantilevered dining room projects outwards over the hillside, while the semi-separate apartment below forms a base for the principal floor of the family home.

Above and right The entrance hallway leads past the family bedrooms towards the main living space, which is open plan, holding the kitchen and dining area to one side and the lounge to the other, while embracing the open views of the hills and the fjord.

Skigard Hytte

A mountain resort retreat

Mork-Ulnes

Kvitfjell
Norway

2019

The cabin is coated in batons of Norwegian spruce, placed diagonally, which help tie the house to its hillside setting bordered with trees while also softening its linear outline.

Norwegian architect Casper Mork-Ulnes and his American wife, designer Lexie Mork-Ulnes, grew up with a great love of skiing. For Casper, skiing was part of family life as a child in rural Norway, while he also developed an early love of the Alps on family ski vacations in Austria and Italy. For Lexie, too, ski culture was part of her upbringing, largely focused on Sugar Bowl in Lake Tahoe, where the couple first met. Skiing has been an important part of their lives together ever since, with their passion for winter sports now shared with their two children and celebrated, above all, in the form of their own family cabin in the Norwegian ski resort of Kvitfjell, to the north of Lillehammer.

'It's so beautiful here and I really fell for it,' says Lexie. 'It's the landscape and the lifestyle, which make it feel so real rather than a story book. We did look at other ski resorts, but none of them had the same kind of feel. It's very different from California, where I grew up skiing, and we decided that it was the only place that we wanted to be. We just fell for the whole package.'[1]

Based in Oslo and balancing a transatlantic portfolio, with projects in North America and Scandinavia, the couple were thinking about building a rural retreat in the mountains when they heard of a site in Kvitfjell from Casper's cousin, who lives on a farmstead nearby. The village itself was transformed into a resort back in the early 1990s during the run-up to the 1994 Winter Olympics in Lillehammer, and has drawn in a number of architects, designers and entrepreneurs over recent decades, including Casper and Lexie Mork-Ulnes.

'We spent time visiting my cousin over the years, skiing in the winter or hiking and fishing in the summer,' says Casper, who studied architecture in the United States. 'There's a real history behind the way that the farms have developed here, or buildings like the stave church, and a knowledge behind the patina and culture. It's all tied to the sense of place and there's a certain authenticity to it. My cousin said you have to come and see this site, so she and her husband drove us up here and we walked through the woods, along the path through the rocks, and saw the view, which was not like anything we had seen before. There was no debate.'[2]

Having bought the land, Casper and Lexie – who have worked closely together for the last ten years – agreed that they wanted to make the most of the setting and the open views across the valley below while touching the earth as lightly as possible. They preserved the existing trees, slotting the cabin between them, and decided to raise the new building above the ground plane on a collection of modestly sized wooden supports, helping to maximize the views but also creating a sheltered undercroft, useful for storing wood and offering a neat shelter for the local sheep and rabbits.

Having created this gently elevated platform, the couple designed a striking entry sequence with a series of steps leading up to a sheltered veranda, which frames a key view of the open landscape while creating a protected, snow-free terrace. The entry to a self-contained guest annexe is to one side and the entrance hallway to the family home is on the other. Here, a boot room and a bathroom sit on one side of the hallway, with bedrooms for the children, Lucia and Finn, on the other, before carrying through to the open-plan living room at the heart of the cabin.

With its sense of openness, as well as the expansive floor-to-ceiling glass windows to either side, the design of this warm and welcoming great room fuses references to California, where the couple used to live, with the ideal of a mountain *rifugio* (refuge) of a kind that the family have fallen in love with during trips to the Italian Alps. Yet the character of this open space, with zones for seating and dining as well as the bespoke kitchen, also draws on the local vernacular, with the use of local pine throughout for the floor and walls. The high, pyramid-shaped ceiling, topped by a skylight, references the local tradition of high, funnel-shaped rooflines seen in mountain farmhouses, where a central chimney helps to serve a fireplace and ventilate the house. These dramatic, high ceilings also feature in other parts of the cabin, including the primary bedroom suite at the far end of the house, lending a sense of space and volume to all the key spaces.

'We wanted the cabin to have a patina that will still be beautiful in a hundred or a hundred and fifty years,' says Casper. 'That's how the Italian mountain *rifugios* feel when you stop there for some food and you go in and there's this amazing patina and a wonderful smell of wood. Even when we go back to Oslo, we can smell the wood of the cabin on our T-shirts, and I really enjoy the way it brings back all these memories of the mountains.'[3]

Here, as with many other recent projects, Casper took the lead on the architectural design, while Lexie led with the interiors, including many integrated elements and a carefully curated mixture of contemporary furniture and Nordic antiques. Pieces such as the vintage Norwegian dining table and chairs sit naturally with the characterful joinery, while the trees and landscape are ever present beyond the windows.

'We didn't want it to be too fancy,' Lexie says. 'That's why we chose the knotty pinewood so that we have a more natural feel rather than a polished edge to the interiors. Everything you see is pine apart from the sauna next to our bedroom, which is aspen, which we chose because otherwise the heat would start pulling the sap out of the pine with the steam.'[4]

The Skigard Hytte, which the couple completed in 2019, takes its name from the diagonal wooden cladding that the couple chose for the exterior of the cabin. The Norwegian spruce batons, seen on local farmstead fences, offer another characterful reference to the local vernacular of a ski-in, ski-out mountain retreat that the couple have found themselves increasingly drawn to as time goes by.

'We would love to turn just a part of it into a little office so that we can spend more time here,' explains Lexie. 'We especially love being here in the winter because this house is a celebration of winter and we always make

Below Steps emerge from the snow and lead upwards to the entrance porch – a covered veranda set within the gently elevated outline of the building, with the main residence to one side and a largely self-contained guest suite to the other.

sure that we come for Christmas. But it works in all seasons and it's also so beautiful in the summer. The sunrises here are unbelievable. I like to wake up before everyone else and just sit on the corner of the sofa and look out of the window and see the sky aflame.'[5]

Below left The interiors include many bespoke and fitted elements but there are also characterful antique pieces in the mix, such as the dining table and the seating around it.

Below The spacious principal suite sits at the far end of the house and includes a sauna, complete with views across the hillside.

Below The veranda offers a semi-sheltered boot room of a kind but also frames a dramatic open vista of the mountains (below). It leads through to the main entrance hall and a sequence of spaces that includes the children's bedrooms and bathroom (below right).

Opposite The double-height living room is spacious enough for a lounge facing the open views, as well as a dining area and kitchen, while the dramatic high ceilings add to the sense of space and volume.

Dalarö House

Opening up to the archipelago

There are striking similarities between the Stockholm Archipelago and the Pacific Northwest coast of America, where architect Tom Kundig and his practice are based. The coastal hinterland between Washington State and the Canadian border, in particular, is punctuated with islands that echo Sweden's eastern coastline to the Baltic Sea in many respects. When an American couple decided to build a summer house on the island of Dalarö, within the inner ribbon of islands upon the archipelago, it seemed a natural choice to approach Olson Kundig.

'This is our first project in Sweden but the Stockholm Archipelago felt very familiar,' says Kundig. 'We have the Sound, also known as the Salish Sea, with countless islands including the San Juan Islands. They are covered in rocky outcroppings and forests, just like Stockholm's Archipelago. I have done a few projects there and they are similar to the Dalarö House in terms of integrating with the existing rocks and connecting to the water.'[1]

Kundig's clients have been regular visitors to Dalarö for twenty years or more, mostly during the summer months when the island – accessible by bridge from the mainland – comes into its own. Houses rarely come up for sale here, but eventually they heard of an irresistible opportunity to buy an existing house on a prime waterside site. More than this, the property also included a small guest house that had once been used by the celebrated Swedish playwright, author and artist August Strindberg, whose work included *The Red Room* (1879) and *Miss Julie* (1888).

The couple realized that the two-storey house could be replaced with a sensitively designed new home, but also that the Strindberg cottage needed to be protected and preserved. The resulting project led to an intriguing dialogue between the new and the old, as well as between architecture and landscape, which Kundig fully embraced. His clients had noted The Pierre,[2] a previous residential project located in the San Juan Islands, where Kundig had explored some similar themes.

'The Pierre and the Dalarö House do share similarities and the most significant to me is how both homes engage with the rocks on their respective sites,' Kundig says. 'Each site has a lot of exposed stone, so it's critical that each home feels nestled into the rock, while allowing that natural geology to become part of the architectural experience. The designs are intentionally quiet to blend into their surroundings and make that connection to the landscape their primary focus.'[3]

Building on the footprint of the original house, Kundig and his clients opted for one storey rather than two, creating a more discreet dwelling that is almost invisible from the neighbouring street, an impression enhanced by the building's green roof and dark timber cladding. The house is essentially composed of three distinct elements, beginning with the entry sequence, where the red front door and its surround offers an echo of the Falun red exteriors of the Strindberg cottage next door. This part of the house holds additional service spaces, as well as a study, while carrying through to the central pavilion, a slightly taller structure with a wall of glass facing the water, as well as connecting with the adjoining terrace and garden.

The pavilion is a generous, bespoke space tailored to the needs of Kundig's clients. A custom kitchen and breakfast nook sit at one end, with the dining area towards the centre, while the substantial lounge has been arranged around the fireplace that is anchored in a wall of raw concrete that contrasts with a palette of predominantly natural materials. Beyond this concrete wall, a hallway leads round to the bedroom wing, which forms the third part of the triptych.

The Strindberg cottage, meanwhile, has been carefully restored and gently updated. It now provides a modest, self-contained guest cottage for visiting family and friends, yet, at the same time, offers an enticing garden room, which also enjoys views of the coast, as well as looking back on the main house. Woven into the landscape, the Dalarö House offers a fully contextual response, even though the surroundings have certain ingredients in common with other Kundig projects halfway around the world.

'The driving force of my work is what makes a place uniquely itself,' says Kundig, 'and architecture has a way of revealing something

The living-room pavilion has been designed to maximize the sense of connection with views across the archipelago, as well as flowing outwards to the adjoining terrace, where the rocky topography still breaks through at times.

Olson Kundig

Stockholm Archipelago
Sweden

2019

about that truth. The Dalarö House was an opportunity to reveal how the rocky site, the water and the Strindberg cottage all come together in this place. It was an opportunity to create a home that directly responds to these elements in a way that encourages the clients to interact with the big views of the water and the quiet moments among the rocks.'[4]

Below The new house is discreetly placed among the rocks and trees while conversing with the original Strindberg cottage to the left, which has been protected and restored.

Opposite The Falun red coating on the cottage served as the inspiration for the colour scheme around the main entrance of the new house, which offers a transitional point between past and present.

Left and opposite
The characterful central pavilion, with its high ceilings, clerestory windows and banks of glass, holds a lounge at one end, a dining zone at the centre and a custom kitchen with an adjoining pantry at the other.

Above and opposite
The principal suite sits at the far end of the new building, enjoying its own sense of seclusion while embracing framed views of the surroundings and the rugged coastal setting.

3-Square House

A family home in the Finnish Lakeland

Sitting on the shores of Lake Saimaa, Studio Puisto's 3-Square House makes the most of its relationship with a captivating landscape. The sculptural cabin sits within the Finnish Lakeland, an extraordinary fusion of woodland and waterways that is particularly rich in natural beauty and wildlife, while offering a therapeutic sense of tranquillity. The single-level house was carefully positioned so that the key living spaces look out across the waters of the lake, while the forest forms a gentle, green backdrop.

'The site's history, the clients' strong feeling and memories, the diverse natural elements, the thick, mystical spruce forest in the background and the beautiful views towards the lake all started guiding the design,' says architect Mikko Jakonen of Studio Puisto, who describes the project as one of the most rewarding of his career. 'From the beginning, it was clear that maximizing the views towards the lake was essential, which was the clients' wish, and the building is elevated on the lake side to create a floating sensation over the water. On the opposite side, we wanted the house to feel more grounded, so the fixed bench in the reading room is elevated to the base level of the forest, providing an experience akin to sitting on the forest floor.'[1]

The project represents a particularly close collaboration between the architects and their clients, a couple with two grown-up daughters. The family has longstanding connections with the setting, and one of the clients spent many summers here visiting his grandparents, who first acquired the lakeside site and built a small summer cabin. Eventually, the family decided to build a new home for use all year round, helped by the acquisition of a small parcel of additional land from a neighbour. Searching for a suitable architect, they came across Studio Puisto's work in a magazine article on its Arctic TreeHouse Hotel in the northern Rovaniemi district of Finland, where connectivity with the surrounding landscape was also a key priority.

By the time that the first conversation began with Jakonen and his team, the family already had a clear idea of what they wanted and how they wanted to live. They were also assisted by the experience of working on their previous homes, which helped the family to formulate a plan for fluid living on one level, with easy flowing spaces leading to terraces and outdoor areas in tune with the surroundings. A sustainable, eco-sensitive building was also a priority for all concerned.

'What interested us about the hotel in the trees,' say the clients, 'was to have a cabin or a cottage standing on pillars so that you don't harm nature. We thought that kind of solution might suit here as well and having just one floor. And it was a must that we should have an ecologically sensitive building and that all the materials should be sustainable. So it's a totally wooden house apart from the roof, which is zinc.'[2]

The house was effectively designed from the inside out, while framing the vistas of the landscape. The family wanted to avoid a procession of separate living spaces, so ideas developed for a more fluid arrangement of living areas arranged around a central core holding the bathrooms and a galley kitchen. Within this square plan, the kitchen, dining and living zones were positioned facing the lake, along with a study and the principal bedroom, while a guest room, library and the reading corner were placed to the rear, all revolving around the central core. Two additional geometrical units on either side hold the garage plus service spaces, and the sauna, with an additional bathroom alongside it. Together this triptych of elements gives the house its name, the 3-Square House, while there is also a second sauna closer to the shore, plus a small guest cottage nearby.

The beautifully detailed and highly crafted interiors feature a range of timbers, including oak parquet floors, walnut and pine for the internal joinery, and oiled alder for the sauna and bathrooms, creating a warm, organic palette throughout. There are many bespoke and integrated elements, including the elegant fitted kitchen, storage units and much of the seating. The underfloor heating is fed by a ground-source heat pump, while the local electricity supply also comes from renewable sources.

As the architects and the owners of the 3-Square House intended, the existing landscape has been carefully respected and

The house floats gently over the hillside looking out over the waters of Lake Saimaa while the woodland forms a vivid, natural backdrop in this restful, rural setting.

Studio Puisto

Southern Savonia
Finland

2019

Above The new house sits lightly within the family compound and among the wooded setting, with a separate summer sauna and a walkway to the dock.

Opposite The residence was designed from the inside out and in response to the family's desire for a fluid, open-plan living space without partitions and focused on the open views of the lake.

preserved, with minimal impact on the site itself. The home is now used through all four seasons, including the winters when the waters of the lake freeze over. It is a family base for hiking, orienteering and kayaking, but it is – above all – a belvedere for enjoying a unique setting loved by multiple generations.

'We have otters in the lake along with cranes and then we have the migrating birds, including the geese that circle round us for fifteen or twenty minutes at a time,' says the couple. 'From every place in the house, you have a view in two directions and you can feel the changes in nature and the seasons, as we are so close. And it's always beautiful; even when it's raining, it's always beautiful here.'[3]

Below and opposite The principal living spaces and family bedrooms revolve around a central service core holding the bathrooms and other amenities, while the free-flowing layout is preserved throughout.

Right The integrated indoor sauna is one of a number of options within the family compound, with two additional saunas also available depending on the season and personal preference.

Greenhouse Home

Living under glass on the family farm

Margit-Kristine Solibakke Klev

Kongsberg
Norway

2019

‘Inside the greenhouse I can grow grapes, apricots, nectarines and peaches’, says Klev, whose two greatest passions are architecture and gardening.

Margit Klev's glass and timber barn sits on the family farmstead, while her parents and siblings also live nearby.

Surrounded by trees and pasture, and sitting on the family farmstead, stands the extraordinary glasshouse where architect Margit Klev and her young family have made their home. Klev created a house within a house, placing her bespoke building inside a vast glass barn, delivered as a kit from Denmark and erected on site in just two weeks. This protective glass shell not only shields the family home inside it, but also shelters an indoor garden and garden rooms, where Klev nurtures the kind of plants and trees that would never usually survive a Norwegian winter.

‘Inside the greenhouse I can grow grapes, apricots, nectarines and peaches’, says Klev, whose two greatest passions are architecture and gardening. ‘I can also grow a lot of herbs around the other plants: parsley, salvia, melissa – herbs that don't grow so well outside. And I can also use the greenhouse to grow small plants from seed that I can plant out in the open later on, in the spring or early summer.’[1]

Klev grew up on the farm, situated in a rural area to the west of Drammen and Oslo, while her mother and father (a land surveyor), as well as her brother and sister all live close by. She initially studied ecology before switching her attention to architecture at Trondheim University, followed by a year in Stockholm. She worked with two practices in Oslo before co-founding her own practice, known as Outline and based in Drammen. The Greenhouse Home was one of her first independent projects and also one of the most personal, shared with her husband, physicist and hydrogen specialist Arnstein Norheim, and their two young children.

Having inherited a parcel of land on the farm, one of Klev and Norheim's greatest wishes was to be able to enjoy the feeling of being outside and immersed in the natural world all year round, including during the harsh Norwegian winters. The solution was a super-sized greenhouse, manufactured by Drivadan in Denmark, and delivered to the site as a vast kit of parts, ready for assembly on a pre-prepared concrete pad. The resulting glass shed is 11.5-metres (38-feet) tall with an area of around 370 square metres (4,000 square feet), while an integrated ventilation system offers natural cooling via roof vents during the warmer months. This glass shell provides a secure and stable environment beneath which Klev created her own bespoke home, the indoor garden and garden rooms.

‘One really important thing was that I wanted to make sure every room in the house had a window that opened on to fresh air and not just into the greenhouse,’ says Klev. ‘So all the bedrooms and key spaces are located to the north or to the east, which also helps keep those rooms cool in the summer. But then I also angled one side of the house holding the most important space, which is the kitchen and where we spend most of our time, so that it fully connects with the greenhouse spaces alongside. The kitchen is really the hub of the house.’[2]

The layout evolved from these key decisions. The spacious kitchen holds the dining area and

a small lounge, all spilling out into the bright and enticing garden zones. A library, his and her offices and two of the four bedrooms are also situated on the ground floor, while upstairs hosts the main sitting room plus the primary suite and an additional bedroom. The flat roof of the house-within-a-house also presented the opportunity to create another shared space: a rooftop terrace ideal for entertaining, but also used as an additional sleeping zone. 'It's usually spring and autumn because it's too cold in the winter and too warm as well as too sunny in the summer,' says Klev. 'Also we have no lights or streetlights on the farm, so it gets completely dark, so we can see the stars through the glass ceiling.'[3]

Sustainability is key, with the farmstead very close to functioning off-grid, with its own biomass plant, water source and a micro hydroelectricity station installed by Klev's father, as well as solar arrays. There is also an element of self-sufficiency to the family's way of living more generally, with Klev growing fruit and vegetables at home, while also sourcing other food and livestock as locally as possible.

'I spend most of my spare time growing vegetables, and for me, sustainability is part of a bigger picture,' says Klev. 'The biomass plant uses wood from the forests around here, which my sister owns, to heat the houses and brings us hot water. My brother's wife has horses, so we use the manure in the vegetable garden. It's all connected. There are big changes in how we experience the house and the garden during the year, but the glasshouse does help to make it possible for us to carry on growing things and keep using these garden spaces all through the winter.'[4]

Opposite The glass superstructure shelters and protects an indoor garden and the family home, which has been created within the outline of the greenhouse.

Below Within this protective enclosure, Klev has been able to create terraces, planted beds and a choice of halfway spaces between inside and outside, as well as a family home.

Opposite and above
The ground-floor living spaces of the family residence, such as the kitchen and dining area, easily connect with the adjoining terraces, where the planting is gently warmed by the enclosure of the glasshouse even in the colder months.

Left and opposite top left
On the roof of the family residence, Klev has created an additional terrace, protected by the pitched roof of the glasshouse, that offers a flexible space for family gatherings and entertaining.

Above and left The sitting room sits at mid-level on a mezzanine looking down to the dining area below, while the principal bedroom suite is positioned alongside, with the extensive use of timber ceilings, floors and joinery giving this part of the house an organic character.

Artist's Barn House

A captivating coastal sanctuary

Studio Bua

Heinaberg
Iceland

2021

Left and overleaf
The retained walls of the former byre form a protective enclosure around the walled garden, as well as framing the approach to the main entrance.

The enchanting coastal landscape around Heinaberg, in the northwest of Iceland, provides a key source of inspiration for artist Gudrún Kristjánsdóttir. The shapes of the mountains and the shadows on the sea find their way into her paintings, but the colours of the landscape – with its rich palette of greens and greys, blues and browns – also seep into her work. More recently, Kristjánsdóttir has been collecting samples of soil and stones and bringing them back to her studio home, overlooking the waters of the Breiðafjörður.

'Ever since I came here, I have felt closer to the elements,' says the artist, who shares her home with her husband, radio broadcaster Ævar Kjartansson. 'I paint, I take photographs and I do drawings based on this place and being here, which becomes more and more important. Then I started to notice these stones on the ground, which had fallen apart and they were red, yellow and other different colours with all of these earth pigments. So I have started to collect them to see if I can use them as pigments in my paintings.'[1]

The couple moved into their combined home and studio by the coast full-time in 2022, having spent many years working on the careful evolution of this former farmstead. They began visiting the area – which was first mentioned in the Icelandic sagas during the thirteenth century – with their son and daughter-in-law. Gradually, the family were seduced by the natural beauty of the remote and rural surroundings, and agreed to buy the former sheep farm, which came with a small house dating back to the 1990s, as well as a handful of much older and largely derelict structures. One of these was a redundant barn, with a lean-to byre attached to it.

'We bought the farm together and then cleaned up the house, which turned out to be better than we had expected,' says Kristjánsdóttir. 'We didn't expect that we would stay here that often, but little by little we started coming more and more because we liked it so much. And then, one day, we took some coffee and sandwiches and had a kind of picnic in the so-called garden in the byre and I said, "this is where we should live".'[2]

Kristjánsdóttir and Kjartansson began working on what was to become a long conversion project, beginning with the task of clearing out the barn, with its decades of farmstead detritus. Their initial contacts with a number of architects were discouraging, but then they discussed the idea of adapting the barn into a new home studio with architect Sigrún Sumarliðadóttir of Studio Bua and her fellow principal Mark Smyth. Fortunately, Sumarliðadóttir already knew Heinaberg and the surrounding area well, as her parents had also bought a farmhouse nearby, which she was involved in renovating and extending, as well as adding a gallery space and a new artist's residence. With all of these ingredients in common, Studio Bua were a natural fit for Kristjánsdóttir and Kjartansson's project.

'I have been fascinated with the ensemble of structures on the land for quite some time and the concrete barn and the ruined walled garden are quite special,' says Sumarliðadóttir. 'They stimulated my imagination and the setting is also very beautiful, with the grassy fields around it that change in colour each season.'[3]

Visiting the site with the couple, the architects soon suggested the idea of adding a new, second storey to the building, while preserving the concrete walls of the original barn on the ground floor. The greatest challenge lay in maximizing every square metre of available space within the outline of the barn for living accommodation plus Kristjánsdóttir's art studio.

'The programme that the clients wanted was quite ambitious,' Sumarliðadóttir says. 'The barn is quite compact as it is and just fits what was required, but the studio also needed to be large enough for Gudrun and then we still needed generous living spaces and a guest room. We also wanted the project to be a light intervention, so the idea of gently inserting a new house inside the original structure came to us. We were also determined not to touch the walled garden, as it seemed very special and we were all keen to maintain its unique quality.'[4]

Given the essential need to create a bespoke studio, Kristjánsdóttir and Kjartansson agreed that she would take the creative lead on the project, working closely on the programme for the project with Studio Bua. A new, two-storey timber-framed structure was slotted into the rectangular holding frame of the barn, with careful consideration given to the positioning of the windows and apertures. Given the extreme winters, the house had to be comprehensively insulated and triple-glazed, with corrugated aluminium cladding for the uppermost level and the roof, as well as underfloor heating served by a ground-source heat pump.

Double-height zones bookend the building at either end, including a high segment for the home studio, topped by skylights. The kitchen, as another creative space, was placed in the centre of the ground-floor plan, with the dining area and the stairwell beyond. The stairs wind their way upwards to the mezzanine living room, where a ribbon of windows frames views of the fjord, while the upper level also holds the principal bedroom, the bathroom and a guest bedroom, which doubles as Kjartansson's podcast recording studio. The byre now offers a tranquil walled garden, partially protected from the elements, while the overall plan has proved a great success for the couple, who are now based at the Artist's Barn House through all four seasons of the year.

'I very much like to cook and paint at the same time, doing these two things together, so I just love it,' says Kristjánsdóttir. 'And the light in the studio is absolutely beautiful, especially in the summer when the sun comes through the window and you get this magical sunlight. I wanted to look at the design of the house as if I was doing an art piece, deciding on every detail, and fortunately both of us are very happy with the way that it has turned out.'[5]

Below Kristjánsdóttir's painting studio sits at one end of the house, including a double-height section that introduces valuable top light from the skylights above.

Left and below The staircase winds upwards from the ground-floor dining room, ascending to the elevated living room, which offers open views of the sea; the guest room alongside also serves as a recording studio.

Above The windows have been carefully positioned within the fabric of the building to frame key views of the meadows, the mountains and the coast, all of which offer sources of artistic inspiration.

Opposite The kitchen sits between the dining room at one end of the house and the painting studio at the other, with artistic endeavours and cooking sometimes overlapping and intersecting.

Villa Gug

A sculptural hilltop statement

'Sometimes you have to do something crazy and bold,' says entrepreneur Mads Peter Veiby, 'otherwise the world would be a very boring place to live.'[1] The house that Veiby and his wife, Rikke Rytter Veiby, have built for themselves and their children near Aalborg is certainly bold. Designed by Bjarke Ingels and his practice, BIG, Villa Gug offers a dramatic, sculptural form within an engaging, open landscape. Yet at the same time, the house is a considered response not only to the setting but also to the specific needs of the family.

'There were a lot of requests,' says Veiby. 'We are a family of four so the house must be liveable and not a museum. It must also serve as an everyday house and be practical. And it's nice to live with the cars. I love cars and consider them to be art as much as sculpture or a painting.'[2]

The cars in question are certainly beautiful in themselves. The collection includes a silver 1959 Porsche 356 Outlaw, along with a handful of other Porsches and Ferraris that might be of museum standard, yet are regularly used by Veiby and his family. Rather than hiding the cars away in a bunker, Veiby wanted the collection to be woven into the design of the house rather than an afterthought. The solution was a fusion of garage and home, provided by Ingels after architect and client connected having both appeared on a television show devoted to influential Danes.

'Here, on the top of a hill, where the local kids go snow tubing in the winter, he wanted to build the house of his dreams for him and his family,' says Ingels, 'and he wanted his cars to be a visible, active part of their house experience. In terms of architecture as portraiture, it is a pure manifestation of a house shaped by the desires of its inhabitants.'[3]

Veiby, who grew up in Aalborg, knows the area well and acquired the site from a local farmer. The hillside setting offers open views across the valley below, with its pastures, fields and woodland, while walking trails thread through the picturesque landscape. Ingels developed the form of the house by taking the idea of a long ribbon, with the car garage at one end and the main living room at the other, and then twisting it into a loop that gradually ascends until the summit of the loop rests on its own base and beginning. The looped ribbon, which ends in a wall of glass facing the landscape, not only fulfilled the multiple requests of the family but also managed to balance connectivity with the landscape and the need for privacy from neighbouring houses at key points.

The cars sit close to the entrance, where a wall of glass looks into a carefully landscaped courtyard garden. A continuous hallway around the rear of the building, finished in white brick, ties together a study, a gym, family bedrooms and other spaces as the loop gently ascends, with each of these spaces looking across the hidden courtyard. Eventually, this 'promenade architecturale' leads to the generously scaled living room, or great room, with the kitchen at one end, a dining area towards the centre and the lounge at the other end, facing the wall of glass that frames the open vista of the valley. Here, again, there are connections with the courtyard garden and an elevated terrace that sits on the roof of the lower portion of the ribbon. A spiral staircase offers a neat shortcut down to ground level and towards the main entrance.

'It is like a string of pearls,' says Ingels.[4] From within, the spaces open up towards the central garden, offering increasingly expansive views as the rooms climb the hill and begin to perceive the distant horizons beyond the roof line. The cars are protected from the outside but visible across the garden from the living spaces and bedrooms. A green roof – punctuated by skylights – softens the outline of the house in the landscape and, while the building is undoubtedly bold, the curvaceous villa is also a very gentle presence within the topography. Dynamic and delightful, the house has fully met the family's expectations.

'When we first saw the design we were choked,' says Veiby. 'This was not what we had in mind but as time went by the idea stuck in our heads and we thought this could actually work. It works for us just as it was designed to do. I love my morning coffee on the terrace or in the living room. I love the view. I can see when my kids get up in the morning. And I can enjoy the cars.'[5]

From above, the winding, ribbon-like form of the house can be fully appreciated, as well as the way in which the building works with the landscape, as seen in its green roof and the rising, topographical courtyard garden.

BIG (Bjarke Ingels Group)

Aalborg
Denmark

2022

Villa Gug

Below The main living room sits at the elevated end of the ribbon, where a wall of glass hovers over the hillside and forms a lens looking out across the open landscape.

Opposite The car gallery forms an integral part of the house, with the family able to enjoy glimpses of the collection from across the courtyard garden; a separate garage alongside the front entrance holds vehicles for daily use.

Above Open views of the surrounding landscape can be fully appreciated from the elevated sitting room, which forms part of an open-plan living space that also includes the dining area and kitchen.

Above From the main entrance, there is a choice of circulation routes, with the entrance hall leading to a spiral staircase that connects directly with the living room above, or, alternatively, a slower journey through the winding hallway that runs alongside the 'string of pearls'.

Opposite, above left and above The glass-sided summit of the spiral staircase from the entrance hall also helps to lightly divide the main living room from the kitchen and breakfast area beyond it.

Left The principal bedroom, complete with a curvaceous Arne Jacobsen Egg Chair, connects with a generously scaled ensuite bathroom positioned a few steps further up the spiralling structure of the building.

Star Lodge

Looking out over the Lysefjord

The Star Lodges are perched on the hillside, looking down towards the winding waters of the Lysefjord below, with the design of each cabin oriented towards this dramatic vista.

The combination of elevation with a panoramic vista creates an extraordinary experience.

The portfolio of work developed by Oslo-based practice Snøhetta over recent years embraces a striking spectrum of settings and scales. There are major cultural projects, including the Lillehammer Art Museum and the landmark Oslo Opera House, which opened in 2008, but there are also modest cabins, refuges and rural retreats. Many of these twenty-first-century escapes sit within precious landscapes, where they become sculptural objects as well as enticing belvederes.

Such is the case with Snøhetta's Star Lodges at The Bolder, where the natural surroundings could hardly be more dramatic. The practice's four cabins sit on a high vantage point, surrounded by mature pines, looking down on to the waters of the Lysefjord, framed by the towering mountains to either side. The combination of elevation with a panoramic vista creates an extraordinary experience, which the Star Lodges were designed to both accommodate and encapsulate.

The Bolder is an immersive micro resort situated around an hour's drive west of the coastal city of Stavanger via the Ryfylke Tunnel, the longest and deepest subsea roadway in the world. It was founded by the Stavanger-based printer and publisher Tom Bjarte Norland, who acquired the site as part of a larger business deal in 2009. The land came with approval for a number of small cottages, which eventually tempted Norland to initiate the new resort, while looking to preserve the rugged beauty of the surroundings as far as possible. Norland began with two modestly sized Sky Lodges, designed by architect John Birger Grytdal, while also approaching Snøhetta about phase two of The Bolder, encompassing a cohesive set of individual cabins perched on the plateau.

'We were overwhelmed by the raw and pristine nature of the site,' says senior architect and project lead Frank Denis Foray. 'Since there was nothing there to begin with, we decided to rent a campervan for the team and stayed there for two nights so that we could better understand the place. We worked with models, drawings and finally directly on site to find the best approach and concept, all the time working with respect for nature. Staying on the site for some days made a big difference in the direction of the design.'[1]

The design programme comprised a quartet of buildings. Of these the three Star Lodges are of a similar size and scale, while the Grand Lodge is more spacious and can accommodate larger groups of guests. Importantly, each of the lodges was carefully sited not only to maximize the impact of the open vista of the Lysefjord but also to create a sense of privacy, avoiding any potential for overlap between the neighbours and enhancing the sense of isolation within this extreme but beautiful setting.

'Every cabin needed a uniqueness,' Foray says. 'We had to find their special relation to the ground and the site, while the feeling of being alone is important, using the vegetation and the landscape as a natural buffer between the cabins. We looked for something that defined shelter, like a nest or a cocoon. At the same time we wanted to give the sensation of floating or flying over the ground.'[2]

While the lodges have individual characteristics, they share similar geometries, resembling wooden crystals sitting lightly on the cliff, with large picture windows facing the fjord. The Star Lodges are two-storey cabins clad in red cedar, resting gently on the rock, and accessed by steel walkways. The main living spaces are on the upper level, featuring an open-plan lounge, dining area and a compact but elegant kitchen, made by the Danish company VIPP, while a large skylight complements the wall of floor-to-ceiling glass framing the panorama.

Downstairs there is a spacious double bedroom, where the bed is angled towards the view over the water and the bridge that spans the two sides of the fjord. Walls, ceilings and joinery are in oak, which not only seems in keeping with the setting but also creates a sense of warmth within the interiors, which also feature furniture by the Norwegian producers Eikund. While the floorprint of the cabins is purposefully modest, the picture windows extend the feeling of space outwards while drawing the landscape inwards.

'Their strong relationship to the surroundings is unique,' says Foray, who has also designed a communal space at The Bolder as part of phase three. 'I have had the chance to stay at The Bolder and the ever-changing weather that you experience through the windows is amazing and offers enough of an argument to go there and visit. You can experience three seasons in one day and the sensation of floating over the ground, on the edge of the cliff, is strong but the human scale and compact solution gives this sense of a warm, safe cocoon.'[3]

Above With each one arranged over two levels, the cabins are gently but securely anchored to the cliff, causing minimal disturbance to the landscape and its ecosystems.

Right The living spaces have been designed around the open views, with VIPP kitchens and appliances, a bespoke dining table and chairs from Eikund.

Above The Star Lodges and the neighbouring Sky Lodges form a cluster of dwellings spread out on the mountain side, with the careful orientation of each one ensuring privacy and seclusion.

Left Clad in red cedar, the Star Lodges adopt a sculptural and almost crystalline form, while the sheets of glass reflect the landscape and the sky.

Above Like the living spaces above, the bedroom level also embraces the open view, with the fitted double bed offering a comfortable platform for enjoying the epic vista.

Villa Bergslia

A fresh fusion of old and new

This curvaceous part of the overall composition consists of a self-contained apartment floating above an integrated garage, while the uppermost level holds a dance studio and workspace.

Perched upon a gentle hillside in a northern neighbourhood of Oslo, bordered by woodland to the rear, Villa Bergslia offers an intriguing dialogue between past and present. The house sits within a part of Oslo known for its early modernist houses from the 1920s and 1930s, and here choreographer Ane Smørås and her husband, writer and journalist Hugo Lauritz Jenssen, acquired a house dating from 1938 designed by the Norwegian architect Ragnar Nilsen. The original, three-storey building has a sophisticated elegance of its own, enhanced by the surrounding garden and the verdant backdrop provided by a protected forest, which runs right up to the rear boundary.

Nilsen, as Lauritz Jenssen later discovered, studied architecture in Trondheim and based himself in Oslo, where he was well respected for his work from both the 1930s and the mid-century period. His extensive portfolio included single-family houses, housing projects and churches, while he was awarded the prestigious Sundt's Prize in 1936 for the design of an apartment building in central Oslo. Just two year later, Nilsen completed Villa Bergslia.

'We liked the idea that the house had character and that it wasn't extensively tampered with,' says Smørås. 'Its interior plan and many of the original details were intact, and the natural light from the windows was beautiful. We felt that the house was a little odd, but in a good way. In Norwegian, it would be called a "skirt and blouse" house – a typology where the first two storeys are made of concrete or brick and the top storey is entirely of wood.'[1]

While the couple both enjoyed and appreciated the house, they also agreed that it had a number of flaws. 'It was a house built in a time when people had less stuff, so the closets were minimal in size and the kitchen was tiny,' Lauritz Jenssen says. 'But every unpractical, unmodern feature adds to the character and soul of the building.'[2]

While the house was in good structural condition, the couple and their son, student and composer Ib Lauritz, all needed dedicated workspaces at the house, while the original kitchen in particular was so limited that it was unsuitable for daily family living. At the same time, the family wanted to create a self-contained apartment for use by visiting family and friends. The solution, they decided, was to add more space but without upsetting Nilsen's modernist villa.

'When we chose to make an extension and an annexe, it was decisive for us to preserve the original house,' says Smørås. 'We wanted to add something that could be in dialogue with the existing building and at the same time challenge it a little bit. But it was never an issue to replace it with something else.'[3]

Architects Siri Moseng and Kaja Poulsen were commissioned to address these concerns, while protecting, preserving and gently updating the original villa. This was, coincidentally, the first of three occasions when Moseng Poulsen (or Mopo) has worked with Ragnar Nilsen's buildings, with other projects including a house from the 1920s and the modernization of one of the architect's post-war office buildings, both in Oslo.

Moseng Poulsen designed new elements positioned at either side of the house, forming two expressive additions that share a similar design language and colour palette. The curvaceous outlines of these new structures, painted in an engaging green that ties in with the woodland backdrop, provide two arms that embrace the original building at the centre, while offering a clearly contemporary intervention.

One of these wings holds a new study at ground-floor level for Lauritz Jenssen, while the couple's son was also provided with a music studio on the other side of the entrance hall. A welcoming kitchen and breakfast room was created on the floor above, united by its yellow units and floors, with the colour choice fulfilling a special request by Smørås. This new addition also helped free up space within the main body of the house, where a more generously scaled, family-sized sitting room is located alongside the dining room.

'There are a lot of old houses that need this kind of help, because they were built for another time when we didn't own that much and we had different ways of living with our families,' says Moseng. 'So it's become something of a mission for us to show that it is possible to work with old houses to make them function for the way we live today.'[4]

The other new element of the house is a detached building, sitting alongside the house, with two floors of accommodation placed above a new garage at road level. A self-contained apartment sits at mid-level of this new structure, occupied by Smørås's mother, while a spacious dance studio and study space for the choreographer was positioned above, on the top floor. Here, the floors are also yellow and the cladding a forest green, while the upper, timber-clad level of the main house was also painted forest green, enhancing the overall composition. With these elements in common, as well as their curvaceous form, these two new wings enable a pleasing conversation with one another, as well as with Nilsen's original building at the centre.

'The sculptural forms provide a sense of having these huge pieces of art on the property and give both us and people passing by something to wonder about,' says Smørås. 'When you build something, you never build it just for yourself – you share it with the society around you. So I think you are obliged to bring something aesthetically pleasing and, at the same time, be humble to the surroundings. Siri and Kaja nailed that and we are confident that our house has made "our" street more interesting.'[5]

Below From the street, the original 1930s house can be seen at the centre, flanked by the two new additions, forming a pleasing triptych of interrelated elements.

Above The new annexe and the extension on the other side of the original house share a common language and a similar aesthetic, with the green siding sitting naturally upon the hillside while the woodland forms a natural backdrop beyond.

Opposite and below Internally, the kitchen and breakfast room within the new extension features a vibrant yellow colour scheme, while connecting directly with the revitalized living spaces in the original house.

Right The work zone in the new dance studio also adopts vivid yellows for the floors and curvaceous fitted furniture, helping to create a sense of cohesion across the various new elements of the enlarged villa.

NOTES

Introduction
Quoted in Norberg-Schulz and Postiglione, 1997, p. 252.

Lilla Hyttnäs, Carl & Karin Larsson, pp. 16–23
1 Quoted in Gunnarsson and Eliasson, 2016, pp. 9–10.

Hvitträsk, Eliel Saarinen, pp. 24–31
1 Quoted in Marjamäki, 2020, p. 82.
2 See Dominic Bradbury and Richard Powers, *The Iconic American House*, Thames & Hudson, 2020.

Villa Mairea, Alvar Aalto, pp. 54–63
1 Quoted in Pallasmaa (ed.), 1998, pp. 71–72.
2 *Ibid.*, p. 8.

Villa Stenersen, Arne Korsmo, pp. 64–71
1 Quoted by the Munch Museum online, www.munchmuseet.no/en/our-collection/the-art-collector-rolf-stenersen.

Juhl House, Finn Juhl, pp. 72–81
1 Quoted in Bundegaard, 2019, p. 217.
2 *Ibid*, p. 171.

Ásmundarsafn, Ásmundur Sveinsson & Einar Sveinsson, pp. 82–87
1 Quoted in Johannessen, 1974, p. 7.
2 *Ibid.*

Utzon House, Jørn Utzon, pp. 88–95
1 Interview with the author.
2 Quoted in Faber, 1969, p. 38.
3 Interview with the author.

Didrichsen House & Museum, Viljo Revell, pp. 96–103
1 Didrichsen, 2023, p. 96.
2 *Ibid.*, p. 93 and p. 103.

Bigaard Sørensen House, Friis & Moltke, pp. 110–117
1 From the Friis & Moltke website: friis-moltke.com

Futuro House, Matti Suuronen, pp. 124–129
1 Quoted in Home and Taanila, 2003, p. 13.
2 *Ibid.*, p. 21.

Villa Schjøtt, Geir Grung, pp. 130–135
1 Geir Grung's *Projects* portfolio, privately published.
2 *Ibid.*

Kukkapuro Studio, Yrjö Kukkapuro, pp. 136–143
1 Kukkapuro-Enbom and Ylä-Mononen, 2017, p. 34.
2 Kukkapuro-Enbom, 2023, p. 68.

Nurmesniemi House & Studio, Antti & Vuokko Nurmesniemi, pp. 144–151
1 Quoted in Nurmesniemi and Kalin, 2006, p. 25.
2 Quoted in Kukkapuro-Enbom and Ylä-Mononen, 2017, p. 53.
3 Quoted in Nurmesniemi and Kalin, 2006, p. 25.

Villa Holme, Sverre Fehn, pp. 152–159
1 Quoted in Peltason and Ong-Yan (eds), 2010, p. 164.
2 Quoted in Yvenes and Madshus (eds), 2008, p. 80.

Árborg Villa, Pk Arkitektar, pp. 168–175
1 Quoted in Kristmundsson et al., 2014, p. 12.
2 Interview with the author.
3 Quoted in Kristmundsson et al., 2014, p. 11.

Fjällbacka House, Gert Wingårdh, pp. 176–183
1 Interview with the author.
2 *Ibid.*
3 *Ibid.*
4 *Ibid.*

Bøe & Møller House, Knut Hjeltnes, pp. 184–189
1 Interview with the author.
2 *Ibid.*
3 *Ibid.*

Villa S, Todd Saunders, pp. 190–199
1 Interview with the author.
2 *Ibid.*
3 *Ibid.*

Manshausen Sea Cabins, Snorre Stinessen, pp. 200–207
1 Interview with the author.
2 *Ibid.*
3 *Ibid.*
4 *Ibid.*

Krokholmen House, Tham & Videgård, pp. 208–215
1 Interview with the author.
2 *Ibid.*
3 *Ibid.*

Villa Birkedal, Jan Henrik Jansen, pp. 216–223
1 Interview with the author.
2 *Ibid.*
3 *Ibid.*

Fleinvær Refugium, Rintala Eggertsson & Tyin Tegnestue, pp. 224–229
1 Interview with the author.
2 *Ibid.*
3 *Ibid.*
4 *Ibid.*

Fanø Summer House, Knud Holscher & Tollgard Studio, pp. 230–237
1 Interview with the author.
2 *Ibid.*
3 *Ibid.*

Villa Sagalid, Sandell Sandberg, pp. 238–245
1 Quoted by Bygg Keramik Rádet online, bkr.se.
2 *Ibid.*

PAN Cabin Three, Espen Surnevik, pp. 246–251
1 Interview with the author.
2 *Ibid.*
3 *Ibid.*
4 *Ibid.*
5 *Ibid.*
6 *Ibid.*
7 *Ibid.*

Jacobsen House, Ósbjørn Jacobsen, pp. 252–257
1 Interview with the author.
2 *Ibid.*
3 *Ibid.*

Skigard Hytte, Mork-Ulnes, pp. 258–263
1 Interview with the author.
2 *Ibid.*
3 *Ibid.*
4 *Ibid.*
5 *Ibid.*

Dalarö House, Olson Kundig, pp. 264–271
1 Interview with the author.
2 See Bradbury and Powers, *Iconic American House*, Thames & Hudson, London, 2020.
3 Interview with the author.
4 *Ibid.*

3-Square House, Studio Puisto, pp. 272–277
1 Interview with the author.
2 *Ibid.*
3 *Ibid.*

Greenhouse Home, Margit-Kristine Solibakke Klev, pp. 278–285
1 Interview with the author.
2 *Ibid.*
3 *Ibid.*
4 *Ibid.*

Artist's Barn House, Studio Bua, pp. 286–293
1 Interview with the author.
2 *Ibid.*
3 *Ibid.*
4 *Ibid.*
5 *Ibid.*

Villa Gug, BIG (Bjarke Ingels Group), pp. 294–301
1 Interview with the author.
2 *Ibid.*
3 *Ibid.*
4 *Ibid.*
5 *Ibid.*

Star Lodge, Snøhetta, pp. 302–307
1 Interview with the author.
2 *Ibid.*
3 *Ibid.*

Villa Bergslia, Moseng Poulsen (Mopo), pp. 308–313
1 Interview with the author.
2 *Ibid.*
3 *Ibid.*
4 *Ibid.*
5 *Ibid.*

BIBLIOGRAPHY

Mikael Bergquist, *Josef Frank: Villa Carlsten*, Park Books, 2019

Mikael Bergquist and Olof Michélsen, *Josef Frank: Falsterbovillorna*, Arkitektur Förlag, 2023

Peter Blundell Jones, *Gunnar Asplund*, Phaidon Press, 2005

Dominic Bradbury, *New Nordic Houses*, Thames & Hudson, 2019

Dominic Bradbury, *Todd Saunders: New Northern Architecture*, Thames & Hudson, 2021

Bjarke Ingels Group, *Formgiving*, Taschen, 2020

Christian Bundegaard, *Finn Juhl: Life, Work, World*, Phaidon Press, 2019

Colin Davies, *Key Houses of the Twentieth Century: Plans, Sections and Elevations*, Laurence King Publishing, 2006

Gunnar Didrichsen, *My Journey to Finland*, Didrichsen Art Museum, 2023

Maria Didrichsen et al., *Viljo Revell: 'It Was Teamwork, You See'*, Didrichsen Art Museum, 2010

Maria Didrichsen, *A Cultural Oasis in Helsinki: The Didrichsen Museum of Art & Culture*, Didrichsen Art Museum, 2019

Tobias Faber, *Arne Jacobsen*, Alec Tiranti, 1964

Tobias Faber, *New Danish Architecture*, Architectural Press, 1969

Charlotte & Peter Fiell, *Scandinavian Design*, Taschen, 2005

Charlotte & Peter Fiell and Magnus Englund, *Modern Scandinavian Design*, Laurence King Publishing, 2017

Per Olaf Fjeld, *Sverre Fehn: The Thought of Construction*, Rizzoli, 1983

Daniel Golling and Kieran Long, *Tham & Videgård, On: Architecture*, Art & Theory Publishing, 2023

Torsten Gunnarsson and Ulla Eliasson, *Carl Larsson's House – From Log Cottage to Total Work of Art*, Carl Larssongården, 2016

Marko Home and Mika Taanila, *Futuro: Tomorrow's House from Yesterday*, Desura, 2003

Gunnar Hoydal, *Janus Kamban*, Listasavn Føroya, 1995

Jari Jetsonen and Sirkkaliisa Jetsonen, *Alvar Aalto Houses*, Princeton Architectural Press, 2011

Matthías Johannessen, *Sculptor Ásmundur Sveinsson: An Edda in Shapes and Symbols*, Iceland Review Books, 1974

Halldor Kiljan Laxness, *Ásmundur Sveinsson*, Helgafell, 1961

Pálmar Kristmundsson et al., *Pálmar Kristmundsson Arkitekt*, Arvinius + Orfeus Publishing, 2014

Isa Kukkapuro-Enbom and Jutta Ylä-Mononen, *Cosy House*, Cosy House Publishing, 2017

Isa Kukkapuro-Enbom, *The Blue Door: Yrjö Kukkapuro Life & Work*, Dodo+Books, 2023

Louna Lahti, *Aalto*, Taschen, 2004

Tomas Lauri et al., *Thomas Sandell – SandellSandberg*, Arvinius + Orfeus, 2010

Robert McCarter, *Aalto*, Phaidon Press, 2014

Jouni Marjamäki, *Hvitträsk*, Finnish Heritage Agency, 2020

Henrik Sten Møller and Vibe Udsen, *Jørn Utzon: Houses*, Living Architecture Publishing, 2006

Christian Norberg-Schulz and Gennaro Postiglione, *Sverre Fehn: Works, Projects, Writings, 1949–1996*, Monacelli Press, 1997

Antti Nurmesniemi and Kaj Kalin, *Antti Nurmesniemi*, Kyriiri Oy, 2006

Juhani Pallasmaa and Tomoko Sato (eds), *Alvar Aalto: Through the Eyes of Shigeru Ban*, Black Dog Publishing, 2007

Juhani Pallasmaa (ed.), *Alvar Aalto: Villa Mairea, 1938–39*, Alvar Aalto Foundation, 1998

Ruth Peltason and Grace Ong-Yan (eds), *Architect: The Pritzker Prize Laureates in Their Own Words*, Thames & Hudson, 2010

Gennaro Postiglione et al, *One Hundred Houses for One Hundred European Architects of the Twentieth Century*, Taschen, 2004

Helen Pitt, *The House*, Allen & Unwin, 2018

Todd Saunders and Jonathan Bell, *Share: Conversations About Contemporary Architecture*, Artifice Press, 2022

Michael Sheridan, *Landmarks: The Modern House in Denmark*, Hatje Cantz, 2014

Félix Solaguren-Beascoa, *Arne Jacobsen: Approach to His Complete Works, 1926–1949*, Danish Architectural Press, Copenhagen, 2002

Félix Solaguren-Beascoa, *Arne Jacobsen: Works & Projects*, Editorial Gustavo Gili, 1989

Carsten Thau and Kjeld Vindum, *Arne Jacobsen: Life & Work*, Danish Architectural Press, 2001

Poul Erik Tøjner, *Knud Holscher: Architect & Industrial Designer*, Edition Axel Menges, 2000

Richard Weston, *Villa Mairea: Alvar Aalto*, Phaidon Press, 2002

Stuart Wrede, *The Architecture of Erik Gunnar Asplund*, MIT Press, 1980

Marianne Yvenes & Eva Madshus (eds), *Architect Sverre Fehn: Intuition – Reflection – Construction*, Oslo National Museum of Art, Architecture & Design, 2008

BIOGRAPHIES

ALVAR AALTO (1898–1976)
Growing up in a rural part of Finland, Alvar Aalto always valued the beauty of the natural world around him. He studied in Helsinki and established his own architectural practice in 1923, marrying architect Aino Marsio the following year. Initially influenced by neoclassicism, Aalto was increasingly attracted to modernism and developed his own unique style, drawing on his love of nature, organic materials and an ergonomic, humanist approach to architecture. Famously, his talents as a designer were applied to furniture and many other areas, including architecture, as seen in such major commissions as the Paimio Tuberculosis Sanatorium of 1933, as well as residential projects, including his own home in Helsinki (1936).
alvaraalto.fi/en/

ERIK GUNNAR ASPLUND (1885–1940)
Pioneering architect Gunnar Asplund was born in Stockholm and educated at the Royal Institute of Technology in the Swedish capital. After travelling in Europe on a scholarship, he settled in Stockholm and opened his own practice in 1911, winning the competition to design the city's Woodland Cemetery with colleague Sigurd Lewerentz in 1914, subsequently built in phases between 1918 and 1940. Other major projects include Stockholm City Library, built between 1920 and 1928, and such residential work as Villa Snellman (1918). Asplund's work fused classicism, Swedish romanticism and early modernism to powerful and original effect.

BIG (BJARKE INGELS GROUP)
With offices in Copenhagen and New York and with projects around the world, BIG (Bjarke Ingels Group) has established itself as one of the most innovative and inventive twenty-first-century practices, known for its form-giving and its ability to challenge convention. The practice was founded by Danish architect Bjarke Ingels in 2006 and is based in Copenhagen, the city where he was born. Born in 1974, Ingels studied at the Royal Danish Academy of Fine Arts and worked with Rem Koolhaas and the Office for Metropolitan Architecture before establishing BIG. The firm's extensive portfolio is wide-ranging and includes housing, offices, infrastructure, museums and cultural projects.
big.dk

SVERRE FEHN (1924–2009)
Norwegian architect Sverre Fehn was born in Kongsberg and studied at the Oslo School of Architecture under the mentorship of Arne Korsmo. He worked with Geir Grung during the early 1950s before winning acclaim for his design of the Norwegian Pavilion at the Brussels World's Fair (1958) and the Nordic Pavilion at the Venice Biennale of 1962. Key cultural commissions include the Storhamarlåven building at the Hedmark Museum in Hamar (1973) and the National Museum of Art, Architecture and Design in Oslo (2008). Fehn was also much respected for his extensive sequence of original villas, beginning with Villa Schreiner in 1963 and including Villa Holme (1998). Fehn was awarded the Pritzker Architecture Prize in 1997.
sverrefehn.info

JOSEF FRANK (1885–1967)
Architect and designer Josef Frank was born in the Austrian spa town of Baden and studied architecture at the University of Technology in Vienna, the same city where he later founded his own architectural practice as well as a home furnishing business known as Haus & Garten. During the 1920s, he designed houses and housing in Vienna and Germany, including a project for the showcase Weissenhof Estate in Stuttgart (1927). Frank began working on architectural projects in Sweden from the late 1920s onwards and eventually settled in Stockholm with his Swedish-born wife, becoming a Swedish citizen in 1939. From the 1940s onwards Frank became better known for his textiles and furniture for the Swedish homeware brand Svenskt Tenn, with many of his designs still in production.
svenskttenn.com/us/en/designers/josef-frank/

FRIIS & MOLTKE
Danish architects Knud Friis (1926–2010) and Elmar Moltke Nielsen (1924–1997) first met as students at the Royal Danish Academy School of Architecture in Copenhagen, graduating in 1950. Friis moved to Aarhus to work with C.F. Møller's practice, while Moltke stayed in Copenhagen working with a number of firms in the capital. They began working together during the mid-1950s after Moltke also settled in Aarhus, formally launching their practice in the city in 1957, prompted by a commission for a new apartment building. They became well known for an extensive sequence of contextual houses, particularly in rural settings, as well as 'landscrapers' such as the Scanticon Training Centre in Skåde (1969). The firm that they founded continues to thrive.
friis-moltke.com

JÁKUP PAULI GREGORIUSSEN (1932–2021)
Born in Tórshavn, capital of the Faroe Islands, Jákup Pauli Gregoriussen trained as an architect at the Royal Danish Academy of Fine Arts in Copenhagen. Returning home and setting up his own practice, Gregoriussen established himself as one of the islands' leading architects from the 1960s onwards, beginning with a wide range of commissions, including a post office, nursing home and primary school. During the 1970s, the architect won a number of major commissions including the Listasavn Føroya art museum (1970) and the National Library (1979). Gregoriussen was also an illustrator, graphic artist and writer, who produced the definitive work on Faroese churches.

GEIR GRUNG (1926–1989)
The son of the early modernist architect Leif Grung, Geir Grung was born in Bergen and trained initially at the Bergen Art School while assisting his father. Following his father's untimely death in 1945, Geir continued his studies at the National Academy of Craft and Art Industry in Oslo, graduating in 1949 and establishing his own practice, based in Oslo, soon afterwards. During the 1950s, he collaborated with Sverre Fehn and his subsequent portfolio included power plants, office buildings, hotels and private houses, as well as the Maihaugen Folk Museum in Lillehammer (1959). Grung was also a naval architect, designing the cruise ship *Song of Norway* and a number of cabin cruisers and sailing yachts.

JAKOB HALLDOR GUNNLØGSSON (1918–1985)
Born in Frederiksberg, Denmark, Jakob Halldor Gunnløgsson was the child of a merchant and an actor. He studied at the Royal Danish Academy School of Architecture in Copenhagen, graduating in 1942. He spent part of World War II in Sweden before returning to Denmark and establishing his own architectural practice in partnership with Jørn Nielsen in 1952. Key projects include Tårnby City Hall (1959) and the Ministry of Foreign Affairs in Copenhagen (1980). He also became a professor and later dean of the architecture school at the Royal Danish Academy.

KNUT HJELTNES (b.1961)
Norwegian architect Knut Hjeltnes was born in Drøbak and grew up in the town of Ås to the south of Oslo. Hjeltnes studied at the Norwegian University of Science & Technology in Trondheim, graduating in 1986. Two years later he began teaching at the Oslo School of Architecture and Design, while establishing his own eponymous practice in the city. Original single-family houses and contextual weekend retreats form the majority of Hjeltnes's extensive portfolio, but he has also designed viewpoints, cafés and the Nordic Artists' Centre in Dalsåsen (1997), as well as a collection of furniture.
hjeltnes.as

KNUD HOLSCHER (1930–2025)
Knud Holscher studied architecture under Arne Jacobsen at the Royal Danish Academy of Fine Arts in Copenhagen, before joining Jacobsen's office and supervising the construction of St Catherine's College at the University of Oxford. In 1968, he became a partner at Krohn & Hartvig Rasmussen (KHR) Architects, as well as teaching at his former architectural school. Later, in 1995, he established Knud Holscher Industrial Design and then Holscher Associates Architects in 1999, balancing architectural commissions with product design of various kinds, as well as lighting and infrastructure. Holscher is well known for his site-sensitive residential projects but also larger commissions such as Odense University (1971 onwards), Bahrain's National Museum (1988), as well as multiple buildings at Copenhagen Airport.

ARNE JACOBSEN (1902–1971)
A multi-talented designer and polymath, Arne Jacobsen preferred to take a holistic approach to his projects, creating a strong sense of synergy between his architecture and the interiors. He trained as a stonemason and then studied in Copenhagen, working with Paul Holsøe before founding his own practice in 1930. His organic, sensitive version of Scandinavian modernism has proved perennially popular, especially his iconic furniture, while key architectural design projects include the SAS Royal Hotel in Copenhagen (1960) and St Catherine's College at the University of Oxford (1966).
arnejacobsen.com

ÓSBJØRN JACOBSEN (b. 1973)
Architect Ósbjørn Jacobsen is a partner at Henning Larsen and the design/studio director of the Danish firm's office in the Faroe Islands. Born in the Faroes, Jacobsen studied architecture in Aarhus, Denmark, and joined Henning Larsen in the year 2000, soon after his graduation. Having worked in Copenhagen, he then moved to Iceland to manage the design and construction of the Harpa Concert Hall and Conference Centre in Reykjavík (2011). Jacobsen returned to the Faroe Islands in 2011, where his projects include Eystur Town Hall (2018), as well as the design of his own family home.
henninglarsen.com

JAN HENRIK JANSEN (b. 1970)
Born in Germany and based in Denmark, Jan Henrik Jansen studied at Leibniz University in Hannover and at the Aarhus School of Architecture. Jansen launched his own eponymous practice in 2012 based in Lyngy, near Copenhagen, with a focus on residential projects and rural escapes. The architect has also designed and built a series of three innovative solo projects on the island of Møn, including Villa Birkedal (2016).
janhenrikjansen.dk

FINN JUHL (1912–1989)
The son of a textile dealer, Finn Juhl studied architecture at the Royal Danish Academy of Fine Arts in Copenhagen, graduating in 1934. He went on to work in Vilhelm Lauritzen's architectural practice, where he also began designing early pieces of furniture. From 1945 onwards, when Juhl established his own atelier, he became better known for his furniture than his architectural work, collaborating with a range of producers including Niels Vodder and France & Søn. Key designs include his Pelican Chair (1940), Poet Sofa (1941) and Chieftain Chair (1949). During the early 1950s, Juhl also began working with Baker Furniture in the United States, who took his work to a much wider and highly receptive audience.
finnjuhl.com

ARNE KORSMO (1900–1968)
Norwegian modernist Arne Korsmo studied architecture at the Norwegian Institute of Technology in Trondheim and graduated in 1926. Two years later, he established a partnership in Oslo with Sverre Aasland, followed by an eponymous practice from 1934 onwards. Korsmo is best known for his innovation in pre-war and mid-century houses including Villa Dammann (1932), Villa Stenersen (1939) and the three houses at Planetveien, including one for himself (1955). Korsmo also taught in Oslo and Trondheim and was an influential member of the Norwegian chapter of the Congrès Internationaux d'Architecture Moderne (CIAM).

YRJÖ KUKKAPURO (1933–2025)
Furniture designer Yrjö Kukkapuro was born in Viipuri in the former Finnish district of Karelia, in the east of the country, which was ceded to Russia in 1945. He studied at the University of Art & Design in Helsinki, graduating in 1958, and established his own design atelier in the capital. Kukkapuro's landmark Karuselli (or 'Carousel') Chair of 1965 secured his reputation, with its dynamic, sculptural form expressed in a fibreglass shell seat on a swivelling steel base. The Karuselli won international attention, with Kukkapuro developing an extensive portfolio of seating and furniture. Later, he turned away from plastics, embracing plywood and organic materials. He also designed his own home studio in Helsinki, completed in 1969.
studiokukkapuro.com

CARL LARSSON (1853–1919) & KARIN LARSSON (1859–1928)
Celebrated Swedish artist Carl Larsson came from a poor Stockholm family, but his talents were noted at an early age and nurtured at the Royal Academy of Fine Arts. He began his career as an illustrator before moving to Paris in 1877, where he met textile designer Karin Larsson (née Bergöö) at a Scandinavian artists' colony. They settled back in Stockholm but eventually moved full-time to Lilla Hyttnäs, their home and garden in Sundborn, to work and raise their large family. The house itself and their work were celebrated, most famously, in Carl Larsson's illustrated book *Ett Home* (*At Home*) published in 1899. As well as being a gifted portrait painter, Carl Larsson was also respected for his monumental frescoes and murals for schools, museums and public buildings.
carllarsson.se

MORK-ULNES ARCHITECTS
The transatlantic practice Mork-Ulnes was founded by Norwegian architect Casper Mork-Ulnes, who was later joined by his American wife, Lexie Mork-Ulnes, who works on the interiors of many of their projects. Based in Oslo and San Francisco, the practice has developed a portfolio of innovative residences, principally in Scandinavia and the United States. Many of their best-known projects are in rural settings and involve highly contextual responses to site and setting.
morkulnes.com

MOSENG POULSEN (MOPO)
The Oslo-based practice Moseng Poulsen, or Mopo, was founded in 2007 by architects Siri Moseng (b. 1973), who studied at the Norwegian University of Science & Technology in Trondheim and Milan Polytechnic, and Kaja Bergliot Poulsen (b. 1974), who is a graduate of the Oslo School of Architecture and the Mackintosh School in Glasgow. The practice began with a series of projects for the Norwegian National Tourist Routes and is now working on a broad portfolio, including conservation projects, housing and private homes.
mopo.no

ANTTI NURMESNIEMI (1927–2003) & VUOKKO NURMESNIEMI (b. 1930)
Following wartime service in an aircraft factory, Antti Nurmesniemi studied at the University of Art & Design in Helsinki, graduating in 1950. He joined Viljo Revell's practice soon afterwards and worked on the interior design of the architect's Palace Hotel project, which led to the design of Nurmesniemi's iconic Palace Sauna Stool of 1952. He went on to establish his own atelier in Helsinki in 1956 and became a much-respected furniture and product designer. There were occasional collaborations with his wife, the celebrated textile designer Vuokko Nurmesniemi, who found fame with her designs for Marimekko in the 1950s and subsequently launched her own eponymous textile and clothing brand.
vuokko.fi/en

OLSON KUNDIG
Born in California in 1954, Tom Kundig grew up in Spokane in Washington State, where his father was an architect. He studied architecture at the University of Washington and became a partner at Olson Kundig Architects, based in Seattle, in 1996. The firm now has five partners, one of whom is the original founder Jim Olson. Kundig's projects include the Montecito Residence (2007), Rolling Huts (2007), Studhorse (2012) and the Tacoma Art Museum (2014), while he has increasingly broadened his portfolio with commissions beyond the United States over recent years, for example, the Dalarö House (2019) in Sweden.
olsonkundig.com

PK (PÁLMAR KRISTMUNDSSON) ARKITEKTAR
Icelandic architect Pálmar Kristmundsson was born in 1955 in the Dýrafjörður district of the country and attended the Danish State School of Architecture in Aarhus, graduating in 1982. This was followed by further studies at the University of Tokyo, as well as a year working in Japan with architect Takefumi Aida. Returning home, Kristmundsson founded PK Arkitektar in Reykjavík in 1986. His work has included private homes, housing, offices, sports clubs and the Icelandic Embassy in Berlin, completed in 1999.
pk.is

VILJO REVELL (1910–1964)
Born in Vaasa, Finnish architect Viljo Revell studied at the Technical University in Helsinki and graduated in 1936. He was part of a brief architectural partnership during the late 1930s before establishing his own independent firm and also assisted Alvar Aalto. During the 1940s, Revell served as the head of the Finnish bureau of reconstruction before resuming work in private practice. He was closely associated with the development of the new neighbourhood of Tapiola, near Espoo, where he designed a collection of innovative buildings. In 1958, Revell won an international competition to design Toronto City Hall in Canada, in association with John B. Parkin Associates, with the project consuming the final years of his life, completing in 1964.

RINTALA EGGERTSSON
Founded by Finnish-born architect Sami Rintala (b. 1969) and his Icelandic colleague Dagur Eggertsson (b. 1965) in 2007, Rintala Eggertsson is based in Bødo in northern Norway and in Oslo. While the practice has developed a collection of projects around these two key locations, the firm also works much further afield, including projects in Finland, Sweden, Iceland and many other parts of Europe. They are much respected for their contextual rural projects in particular, including the Panorama Landscape Hotel & Forest Spa in Tahko, Finland (2023) and Fleinvær Refugium in northern Norway (2017).
ri-eg.com

ELIEL SAARINEN (1873–1950)
Born in Finland, Eliel Saarinen studied fine art and architecture. Working with Herman Gesellius and Armas Lindgren, Saarinen designed a series of major works in and around Helsinki during the early years of the twentieth century, including Helsinki Central Railway Station (1906) and the National Museum of Finland (1910). Then, in the early 1920s, he emigrated to the United States with his wife, Loja, and their children. There, he established the Cranbrook Academy of Art, designing many of its key buildings and becoming president in 1932. In later years, he also collaborated with his son Eero Saarinen on multiple commissions and designed a series of landmark churches.

SANDELL SANDBERG
Thomas Sandell's first career was in the military, where he served as an officer with the Swedish armed forces. Sandell (b. 1959) applied to architecture school as a mature student and studied in Stockholm, graduating from the Royal Institute of Technology in 1990. Initially, he launched a solo practice focused on interior architecture and furniture design. Over time, the practice evolved and grew, becoming Sandell Sandberg following the arrival of Ulf Sandberg, and their portfolio now embraces a range of scales and typologies. The practice is well known for its standalone family homes and housing projects, but has also designed schools, hotels and collections of furniture.
sandellsandberg.se

TODD SAUNDERS (b. 1969)
Based in Bergen, Norway, Canadian architect Todd Saunders was born in Gander, Newfoundland. He studied at the Nova Scotia College of Art & Design and then McGill University in Montreal, followed by a period of travelling and research, particularly within Northern Europe, and eventually settled in Bergen. Saunders established his firm, Saunders Architecture, in 1998 and has balanced commissions across Scandinavia and North America. As well as his many residential projects, Saunders is well known for his work on resorts and rural escapes, including the celebrated Fogo Island Inn (2013).
saunders.no

SNØHETTA
Principally based in Oslo and New York, Snøhetta was founded by Norwegian architect Kjetil Trædal Thorsen (b.1958) and his American colleague Craig Edward Dykers (b.1961) in 1989. Named after a Norwegian mountain range, the practice was launched on the back of its competition-winning entry for the Bibliotheca Alexandrina in Egypt, which was completed in 2001. The firm has become increasingly multinational, but retains a strong and significant portfolio in Norway, where its many projects include the Norwegian National Opera & Ballet in Oslo (2008) and its ongoing work at The Bolder resort in Stavanger. More recently, the practice has completed the Shanghai Grand Opera House in China (2025).
snohetta.com

MARGIT-KRISTINE SOLIBAKKE KLEV (b. 1978)
Norwegian architect Margit-Kristine Solibakke Klev studied at the Norwegian University of Science & Technology in Trondheim, graduating in 2008. She went on to work with Filter Arkitekter and then Jostein Rønsen Arkitekter in Oslo, before co-founding her own firm, Outline Arkitektur, based in the city of Drammen, along with two other partners, Nicolas Jury and Leif Bergersen. Outline's projects include houses, housing, cabins and infrastructure projects, while Klev also designed the Greenhouse Home (2019) on her family farm near Drammen.
outline-ark.no

SNORRE STINESSEN (b.1974)
Norwegian architect Snorre Stinessen was born in the Arctic North and studied at the National University of Science & Technology in Trondheim and Milan Polytechnic. He founded his own practice in 2005, based in Tromsø and Lyngen, and has become well known for his residential work and his northern resorts, including multiple projects at Manshausen, near Bødo, and the Aurora Resort in the Lyngen Alps.
bystinessen.com

STUDIO BUA
Founded in 2017 and principally based in London, Studio Bua was established by the Icelandic architect Sigrún Sumarliðadóttir (b.1980) and Mark Smyth (b.1985), who was born in Ireland. The two principals both studied at the Technical University in Delft, graduating on 2010, and have extensive experience of working in both Scandinavia and Britain. Many of Studio Bua's recent residential projects are focused on the UK and Iceland, including the Artist's Barn House (2021) in rural Heinaberg.
studiobua.com

STUDIO GRANDA
Studio Granda was established in Reykjavík in 1987 by the Icelandic architect Margret Harðardóttir (b.1959) and her English colleague Steve Christer (b.1960), who both trained at the Architectural Association in London. Harðardóttir had previously studied at the University of Edinburgh and Christer at the University of Newcastle. Their projects, which are mostly in Iceland, include new residences and renovations, but also infrastructure, commercial offices and, more recently, parliamentary offices in Reykjavík (2024), a number of which involved collaborations with Icelandic artists of various disciplines.
studiogranda.is

STUDIO PUISTO
Finnish architectural practice Studio Puisto, based in Helsinki, was co-founded in 2010 by Mikko Jakonen, Emma Johansson, Sampsa Palva, Heikki Riitahuhta and Willem van Bolderen. The practice is well known for its work in the hotel and hospitality sector, including the Arctic TreeHouse Hotel & Restaurant (2016/17) and other rural resorts. The firm is also respected for its contextual, site-specific residential projects.
studiopuisto.fi

ESPEN SURNEVIK (b.1973)
Norwegian architect Espen Surnevik studied at the Oslo School of Architecture, where he now teaches, graduating in the year 2000. He founded his own eponymous practice in 2011, based in Oslo, earning particular acclaim for his design of Våler Church, completed in 2015, following his success in an international design competition. Surnevik also designed Porsgrunn Church (2019) to replace a house of worship lost in a fire and is highly respected for his vacation houses, including the PAN Cabins (2018) in Åsnes.
espensurnevik.no

MATTI SUURONEN (1933–2013)
Finnish architect Matti Suuronen was born in Lammi in the south of Finland and studied at the University of Technology in Helsinki, graduating in 1961. Having worked with a number of architectural practices during his studies, Suuronen decided to open his own firm after graduation, designing his own home and studio in Espoo. His work includes houses, housing, offices and service stations, yet he is best known as the inventor of the Futuro House, first produced by Polykem in 1968, and associated prefabricated, modular designs such as the Venturo (1971), also made of reinforced fibreglass.

ÁSMUNDUR SVEINSSON (1893–1982)
Icelandic artist and sculptor Ásmundur Sveinsson was born in rural Kolsstadir and initially studied at the Technical College of Iceland in Reykjavík, as well as serving an apprenticeship with sculptor Ríkarðour Jónsson. From 1919 onwards he continued his studies in Copenhagen, Stockholm and Paris before eventually returning home in 1929. He went on to become the best-known Icelandic sculptor of his generation, fusing modernism with reference to folklore, myth and the vernacular. His interest in monumentality and architecture led to the creation of his own home studio, Ásmundarsafn, in Reykjavík, designed with the assistance of Einar Sveinsson.
listasafnreykjavikur.is/en/asmundarsafn-en

EINAR SVEINSSON (1906–1973)
Having studied architecture at the Technical University of Darmstadt in Germany, Icelandic architect Einar Sveinsson returned home in 1932 and became one of the best-known proponents of modernist architectural design in the country. Just two years later, in 1934, he was appointed Reykjavík's city architect, with a wide range of pre- and post-war projects that included housing, schools, hospitals and swimming pools. He assisted the celebrated Icelandic sculptor Ásmundur Sveinsson with the design of his studio, also known as 'The Shed', at his Reykjavík home, Ásmundarsafn.

THAM & VIDEGÅRD
Swedish architects Bolle Tham (b. 1970) and Martin Videgård (b. 1968) were both born in Stockholm and graduated from the KTH Royal Institute of Technology School of Architecture, following studies at various other institutions. They founded Tham & Videgård Arkitekter in 1999, based in Stockholm, which has become highly respected for the design of individual, site-specific homes, including a number of projects on the islands of the archipelago. Their portfolio also features housing, campus buildings and cultural commissions, including the Kalmar Museum of Art (2008) and Malmö Museum of Modern Art (2010), as well as the Treehotel in Harads (2010).
thamvidegard.se

TOLLGARD STUDIO
Designer Staffan Tollgård was born in Stockholm in 1972 and studied for a post-graduate diploma at the Inchbald School of Design in London, following his first career as a film maker. Having worked initially with Rabih Hage Studio, he co-founded Tollgard Studio in 2005 with his partner Monique Tollgård. As well as its residential work in Britain and Scandinavia, Tollgard Studio's portfolio includes projects in Portugal, the United States and other parts of the world.
tollgardstudio.com

TYIN TEGNESTUE
Norwegian practice Tyin Tegnestue was based in Trondheim, led by principals Yashar Hanstad, Andreas Gjertsen and Ørjan Nyheim. Founded in 2008, the firm co-designed the Fleinvær Refugium in conjunction with Rintala Eggertsson, as well as other projects in Norway, Scandinavia and beyond. The firm disbanded in 2019, with the principals going on to pursue other projects.

JØRN UTZON (1918–2008)
The son of a naval architect, Jørn Utzon was born in Copenhagen and studied at the city's Royal Academy of Fine Arts. He worked briefly with Erik Gunnar Asplund and with Alvar Aalto in Finland before establishing his own practice in Denmark in 1950. In 1957, Utzon won the Sydney Opera House competition, although the landmark project proved controversial and Utzon eventually resigned from the job in 1966. The building was declared a World Heritage site in 2007, and Utzon was awarded the Pritzker Architecture Prize in 2003. Other key projects include his Kingo Courtyard Housing at Helsingør, Denmark, completed in 1958, and Bagsværd Church near Copenhagen (1976).

GERT WINGÅRDH (b. 1951)
Born in Skövde in Sweden, Gert Wingårdh spent part of his childhood in Gothenburg and studied at Gothenburg University and the Chalmers University of Technology, graduating in 1975. Wingårdh established his eponymous practice in 1977, developing his office from small beginnings, assisted by the attention granted to his prize-winning Öijared Country Club in 1988. While Wingårdh is highly respected for his residential work and resorts, the portfolio also encompasses major projects in the fields of education and culture, as well as commercial ventures. One of his most prominent works is his sculptural control tower for Stockholm's Arlanda Airport in Sweden (2001).
wingardhs.se

GAZETTEER

This listing contains concise contact details for houses that are accessible to the public, either for visits, special events or holiday rental. Access to the properties below varies considerably, so always ensure that you contact the institution in question to make arrangements and secure bookings before visiting. Any houses that are featured in this book but are not listed below are strictly private and not open to the public. The owners politely request that their privacy is respected at all times.

ÁSMUNDERSAFN – ÁSMUNDUR SVEINSSON & EINAR SVEINSSON
Sigtún 105, Reykjavík, Iceland
listasafnreykjavikur.is/en/asmundarsafn-en

DIDRICHSEN HOUSE & MUSEUM – VILJO REVELL
Kuusilahdenkuja 1, 00340, Helsinki, Finland
didrichsenmuseum.fi/en

FUTURO HOUSE – MATTI SUURONEN
WeeGee Exhibition Centre, Ahertajantie 5, 02100, Espoo, Helsinki, Finland
espoo.fi/en/exhibition-centre-weegee

VILLA BIRKEDAL – JAN HENRIK JANSEN
Møn, Denmark
urlaubsarchitektur.de/en/birkedal/

HVITTRÄSK – ELIEL SAARINEN
Hvitträskinitie 166, Kirkkonummi, 02440 Luoma, Finland
kansallismuseo.fi/en/hvittraesk

JUHL HOUSE – FINN JUHL
Ordrupgaard, Vilvordevej 110, 2920 Charlottenlund, Copenhagen, Denmark
ordrupgaard.dk/en/

LILLA HYTTNÄS – CARL & KARIN LARSSON
Carl Larrson-gården, Carl Larssons väg 12, 79015 Sundborn, Sweden
carllarsson.se/en/

MANSHAUSEN SEA CABINS – SNORRE STINESSEN
Steigen, Norway
manshausen.no

PAN CABIN – ESPEN SURNEVIK
Joger Hansens Veg, 2280 Gjesåsen, Åsnes, Hedmark, Norway
panhytter.no/en/

FLEINVÆR REFUGIUM – RINTALA EGGERTSSON & TYIN TEGNESTUE
Fordypningsrommet, Fleinvær, Norway
thearctichideaway.com

STAR LODGE – SNØHETTA
The Bolder, Ryfylkevegen 259, 4110 Forsand, Stavanger, Norway
thebolder.no

VILLA MAIREA – ALVAR AALTO
Pikkukoivukuja 20, 29600 Noormarkku, Finland
villamairea.fi/en/

VILLA STENERSEN – ARNE KORSMO
Tuengen Allé 10C, 0374, Oslo, Norway
nasjonalmuseet.no/en/visit/locations/villa-stenersen/

INDEX

ACKNOWLEDGMENTS

The authors would like to express their sincere gratitude to all of the home owners, guardians, architects and designers who have assisted in the production of this book. We would also like to extend our particular thanks to Faith Bradbury & family, Oscar Brehmer, Mere Eskolin, Helsinki Partners, Carria Kania, Isa Kukkapuro-Enbom, Juergen Junker, Leena Karppinen, Frantz Longhi, Danielle Miller & family, Louis Nixon, Steven Salt, Francesca Semenzato, Zrinka Twingler, Simon Willmoth and the staff of the RIBA Library, along with Lucas Dietrich, Fleur Jones, Yasmin Gapper, Catherine Hooper, Jane Cutter and the rest of the team at Thames & Hudson.

For all of their valued assistance and support, special thanks are due to:

SCANDIC HOTELS
scandichotels.com

In loving memory of my wonderful Svigermor, Helene Henriksen-Miller

First published in the United Kingdom in 2025 by Thames & Hudson Ltd, 6–24 Britannia Street, London WC1X 9JD

First published in the United States of America in 2026 by Thames & Hudson Inc., 500 Fifth Avenue, New York, New York 10110

Designed by Therese Vandling

EU Authorized Representative: Interart S.A.R.L.
19 rue Charles Auray, 93500 Pantin, Paris, France
productsafety@thameshudson.co.uk
interart.fr

A CIP catalogue record for this book is available from the British Library

Library of Congress Control Number
2025944602

ISBN 978-0-500-02623-6
01

Printed and bound in China by RR Donnelley